Teach Yourself

VISUALLY™

Adobe® Dreamweaver® CS5

Visual

by Janine Warner

WILEY

Wiley Publishing, Inc.

Teach Yourself VISUALLY™
Adobe® Dreamweaver® CS5

Published by
Wiley Publishing, Inc.
10475 Crosspoint Boulevard
Indianapolis, IN 46256
www.wiley.com

Published simultaneously in Canada

Library of Congress Control Number: 2010929317

ISBN: 978-0-470-61262-0

Manufactured in the United States of America

10 9 8 7 6 5 4 3 2 1

Trademark Acknowledgments

Contact Us

For general information on our other products and services please contact our Customer Care Department within the U.S. at 877-762-2974, outside the U.S. at 317-572-3993, or fax 317-572-4002.

For technical support, please visit www.wiley.com/techsupport.

Wiley Publishing, Inc.

Sales

Contact Wiley
at (877) 762-2974 or
fax (317) 572-4002.

Credits

Executive Editor
Jody Lefevere

Project Editor
Dana Rhodes Lesh

Technical Editor
Lee Musick

Copy Editor
Dana Rhodes Lesh

Editorial Director
Robyn Siesky

Business Manager
Amy Knies

Senior Marketing Manager
Sandy Smith

Vice President and Executive Group Publisher
Richard Swadley

Vice President and Executive Publisher
Barry Pruett

Project Coordinators
Sheree Montgomery
Lynsey Stanford

Graphics and Production Specialists
Joyce Haughey
Andrea Hornberger
Jennifer Mayberry

Quality Control Technician
Lauren Mandelbaum

Proofreading and Indexing
Estalita Slivoskey
Evelyn Wellborn

Screen Artists
Ana Carrillo
Jill A. Proll
Ronald Terry

Illustrators
Ronda David-Burroughs
Cheryl Grubbs

About the Author

Janine Warner's best-selling books and videos on Web design have won her an international following and earned her speaking and consulting engagements around the world. Since 1996, she's written more than a dozen books about the Internet, including the best-selling *Dreamweaver For Dummies, Web Sites Do-It-Yourself For Dummies,* and *Mobile Web Design For Dummies.* Janine is also the host of more than 50 hours of Web design training videos on Adobe Dreamweaver and CSS.

Since 2001, Janine has run her own business as a writer, speaker, and consultant. She has worked on large and small Web site projects, and she is the creator of the Web design training site DigitalFamily.com. Janine has also been a part-time faculty member at both the University of Miami and the University of Southern California Annenberg School for Communication.

Janine started her career as a journalist, and her articles and columns have appeared in a variety of publications, including the *Miami Herald, Shape Magazine,* and *Point Reyes Light.* She's also a regular columnist for *Layers Magazine.*

From 1994 to 1998, Janine ran Visiontec Communications, a Web design firm in Northern California, where she worked for a diverse group of clients including Levi Strauss & Co., AirTouch International, Beth's Desserts, and many other small and medium-sized businesses. From 1998 to 2000, she worked for the *Miami Herald,* first as its online managing editor and later as director of new media. She left that position to serve as director of Latin American operations for CNET Networks, an international technology media company.

A popular speaker at conferences and events throughout the United States, Janine speaks about topics such as Web design, Dreamweaver, and blogging, and she also does keynotes on Internet trends, including social media, marketing, and online reputation.

Janine has had the honor of judging International Internet contests, including serving as a judge for the Knight News Challenge grant program, and the Arroba de Oro Latin American Internet awards. She is a volunteer consultant for the LA Unified School district and helped create an Internet literacy program for high school students in Central America called Operación Red (Operation Network).

Janine currently lives with her husband in Southern California.

Author's Acknowledgments

Special thanks to some of the Web designers and photographers whose work is featured in this book, including David LaFontaine, Davi Cheng, Stephanie Kjos, and Lynn Garrett.

Thanks to my entire family, most notably my adorable nieces and nephew, Mikayla, Savannah, Jessica, and Calahan, whose photos appear in the Chocolate Game Web site.

And finally, thanks to the entire team at Wiley Publishing, especially my editors, Dana Lesh and Jody Lefevere.

How to Use This Book

Who This Book Is For

This book is for readers who have never used Dreamweaver to create Web sites, as well as those who have some experience and want to learn the newest features in version CS5 of this powerful program. All you need to get started is a basic understanding of how to surf the Web and a desire to learn to create your own Web sites.

The Conventions in This Book

① Steps

This book uses a step-by-step format to guide you easily through each task. Numbered steps are actions you must do; bulleted steps clarify a point, step, or optional feature; and indented steps give you the result.

② Notes

Notes give additional information — special conditions that may occur during an operation, a situation that you want to avoid, or a cross-reference to a related area of the book.

③ Icons and Buttons

Icons and buttons show you exactly what you need to click to perform a step.

④ Tips

Tips offer additional information, including warnings and shortcuts.

⑤ Bold

Bold type shows command names, options, and text or numbers you must type.

⑥ Italics

Italic type introduces and defines a new term.

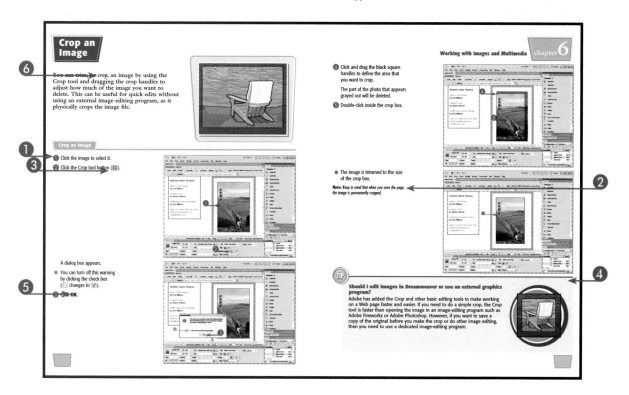

Table of Contents

chapter 3 Exploring the Dreamweaver Interface

chapter 4 Working with XHTML

Table of Contents

chapter 5   Formatting and Styling Text

chapter 6   Working with Images and Multimedia

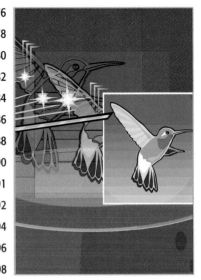

chapter 7 Creating Hyperlinks

chapter 8 Editing the Table Design in a Web Page

Table of Contents

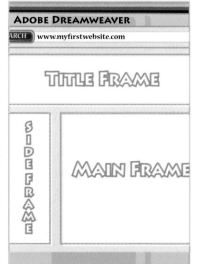

chapter 11 Using Library Items and Templates

chapter 12 Creating and Applying Cascading Style Sheets

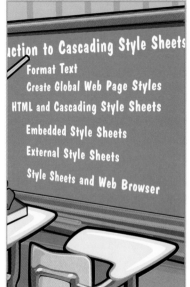

Table of Contents

chapter 13 Designing a Web Site with CSS

chapter 14 Publishing a Web Site

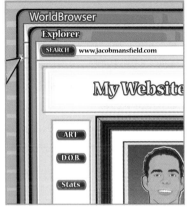

chapter **15** Maintaining a Web Site

chapter **16** Adding Interactivity with Spry and JavaScript

CHAPTER 1

Getting Started with Dreamweaver

This chapter describes the World Wide Web, introduces the different types of information that you can put on a Web site, and shows you how to get started with Dreamweaver.

Introducing the World Wide Web

You can use Dreamweaver to create, edit, and publish pages on the World Wide Web.

The World Wide Web

The *World Wide Web* — or simply the *Web* — is a global collection of documents located on Internet-connected computers. You can access the Web by using a Web browser, such as Internet Explorer, Safari, or Firefox. Web pages are connected to one another by hyperlinks that you can click.

A Web Site

A *Web site* is a collection of linked Web pages stored on a Web server. Most Web sites have a *home page* that describes the information located on the Web site and provides a place where people can start their exploration of the Web site. A good Web site includes links that make it easy to find the most important content on the site.

Dreamweaver

Dreamweaver is a program that enables you to create and edit Web pages with hyperlinks, text, images, and multimedia. You can design Web pages on your computer and then, when you are finished, use Dreamweaver to transfer the finished files to a Web server where others can view them on the Web.

HTML and XHTML

Hypertext markup language (HTML) is the formatting language that is used to create Web pages. The *extensible hypertext markup language* (XHTML) is a stricter version of HTML that meets today's Web standards. You can use Dreamweaver to create Web pages without knowing HTML because Dreamweaver writes the HTML or XHTML for you behind the scenes.

A Web Server

A *Web server* is a computer that is connected to the Internet and has software that serves Web pages to visitors. Each Web page that you view in a Web browser on the World Wide Web resides on a Web server somewhere on the Internet. When you are ready to publish your pages on the Web, you can use Dreamweaver to transfer your files to a Web server.

A Web Browser

A *Web browser* is a program that can download Web documents from the Internet, interpret HTML, and then display the Web page text and any associated images and multimedia. Popular Web browsers include Microsoft Internet Explorer, Mozilla Firefox, Apple Safari, and Google Chrome.

Explore the Many Ways to Design a Web Page

In the early days of the Internet, Web design was easy but boring. Today, there are many more ways to design Web pages, but first you have to decide which approach is best for your site. Here are a few of the options that you can choose.

Text and Images

Inserting text and images into a Web page is the simplest design option. Dreamweaver makes it easy to add images and text and to change the size, color, and font of the text on your Web page. It also makes it easy to organize text into paragraphs, headings, and lists, as well as change alignment. However, if you want to create a more complex design, you need to use one of the other options described in this section.

Tables

Tables used to be a popular choice for creating page designs. By merging and splitting table cells and turning off the border setting, you could create complex page layouts. Today, designing with cascading style sheets is the best option, and tables are no longer recommended, except for formatting tabular data, such as the kind of information you would find in a spreadsheet program or a database.

Frames

On Web sites designed with frames, the browser window is divided into rectangular frames, and a different Web page loads into each frame. Dreamweaver offers visual tools for building frame-based Web sites, but frames are no longer recommended for most Web designs because only the first page of a frameset can be bookmarked, frames are harder to optimize for search engines, and navigating around frames can be confusing to visitors.

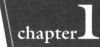
AP Divs

Dreamweaver's AP Divs, called *layers* in earlier versions of Dreamweaver, use absolute positioning to create "boxes" that you can use to position images, text, and other content on a page. AP Divs are very intuitive to use: You just click and drag to create a box anywhere on a Web page. Their biggest limitation is that you cannot center a design created with AP Divs, a common trick for accommodating different screen sizes. Another limitation is that, although they seem to give you precise design control, their display can vary dramatically from browser to browser.

CSS Layouts

Many professional Web designers today recommend creating page layouts using cascading style sheets (CSS). Although AP Divs are technically CSS layouts, they receive very special treatment in Dreamweaver and have some very significant limitations. When designers refer to CSS layouts, they generally mean designs that do not use absolute positioning — or that use it very sparingly. Using CSS is one of the most challenging Web design options, but it brings some powerful benefits, such as greater accessibility and flexibility, which can help your site look better to more people on a greater range of devices. When used effectively, pages designed with CSS are also faster to download and easier to update.

Adobe Flash

Some of the "flashiest" sites on the Web have been created using Adobe Flash, a vector-based design program that you can use to create animations and highly advanced interactive features. Although you can use Dreamweaver to add Flash files to your Web pages and to create some basic Flash elements, such as Flash buttons, you should know that many of the most elaborate multimedia sites on the Web were created using Flash and Dreamweaver.

Dynamic Web Sites

At the highest end of the Web design spectrum, you can connect a Web site to a database, extensible markup language (XML) files, or another data source to create highly interactive sites with features such as shopping carts, blogs, discussion boards, and more. Database-driven sites are especially useful when a Web site grows to more than 100 pages or so because they are much more efficient to update.

Carefully planning your pages before you build them can help to ensure that your finished Web site looks great and is well organized. Before you start building your Web site, take a little time to organize your ideas and gather the materials that you will need.

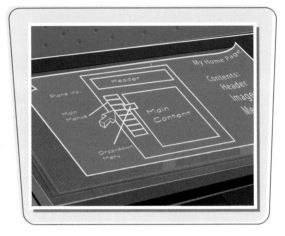

Organize Your Ideas

Build your Web site on paper before you start building it in Dreamweaver. Sketching out a Web site map, with rectangles representing Web pages and arrows representing links, can help you to visualize the size and scope of your project. Use sticky notes if you want to move pages around as you plan your Web site.

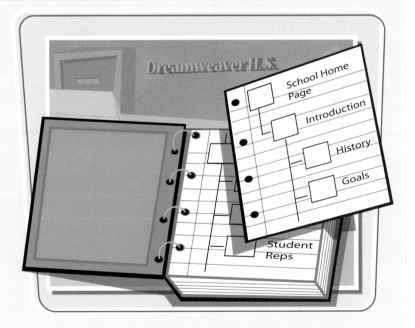

Gather Your Content

Before you start building your Web site, gather all the elements that you want to use. This process may require writing text, taking photos, and designing graphics. It can also involve producing multimedia content, such as audio and video files. Gathering all your material together in the beginning makes it easier for you to organize your Web site when you start building it in Dreamweaver.

Define Your Audience

Identifying your target audience can help you to decide what kind of content to offer on your Web site. For example, you may create a very different design for small children than for adults. It is important to know whether visitors are using the latest Web browser technology and how fast they can view advanced features, such as multimedia.

Host Your Finished Web Site

To make your finished Web site accessible on the Web, you need to store, or *host*, it on a Web server. Most people have their Web sites hosted on a Web server at a commercial Internet service provider (ISP) or at their company or university.

Start Dreamweaver on a PC

You can start Dreamweaver on a PC and begin building pages that you can publish on the Web. You first need to purchase and install Dreamweaver if you do not have it already. You can also download a free trial version from Adobe's Dreamweaver Web page, www.adobe.com/dreamweaver.

Start Dreamweaver on a PC

① Click **Start**.

② Click **All Programs**.

③ Click **Adobe Dreamweaver CS5**.

Note: Your path to the Dreamweaver application may be different, depending on how you installed your software and your operating system.

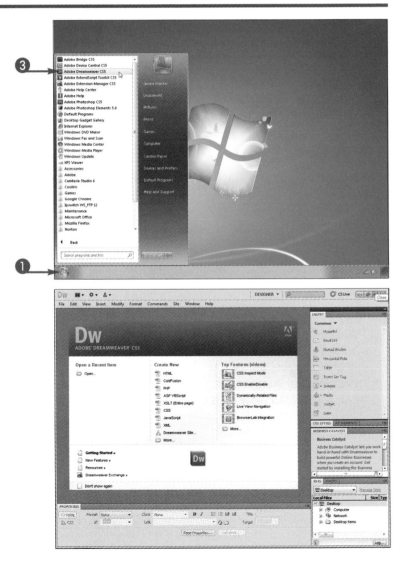

The Dreamweaver start screen appears.

Just before Dreamweaver starts, you may be prompted with a dialog box that gives you the option of making Dreamweaver the default editor for many kinds of file types, including CSS, XML, and PHP. If you want to open these kinds of files automatically in Dreamweaver, click **OK**.

You can start Dreamweaver on a Macintosh and begin building pages that you can publish on the Web. You first need to purchase and install Dreamweaver or download a free trial version from Adobe's Dreamweaver Web page, www.adobe.com/dreamweaver.

Start Dreamweaver on a Macintosh

1 Double-click your hard drive icon.

2 Click **Applications**.

3 Click **Adobe Dreamweaver CS5**.

Note: The exact location of the Dreamweaver folder depends on how you installed your software.

4 Double-click **Adobe Dreamweaver CS5.app**.

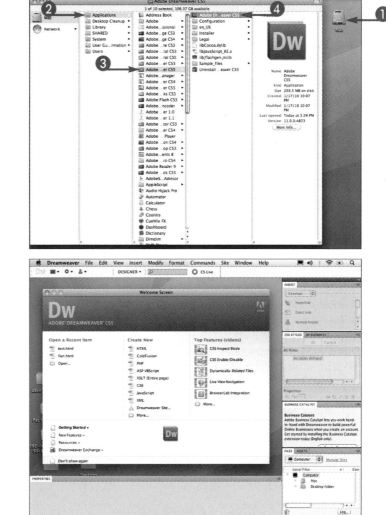

The Dreamweaver start screen appears.

Just before Dreamweaver starts, you may be prompted with a dialog box that gives you the option of making Dreamweaver the default editor for many kinds of file types, including CSS, XML, and PHP. If you want to open these kinds of files automatically in Dreamweaver, click **OK**.

Tour the Dreamweaver Interface on a PC

Dreamweaver CS5 on a PC features a variety of windows, panels, and inspectors.

Menus

Contain the commands for using Dreamweaver. Many of these commands are duplicated within the windows, panels, and inspectors of Dreamweaver.

Toolbar

Contains shortcuts to preview and display features and a text field where you can specify the title of a page.

Insert panel

Provides easy access to common features. There are several different Insert panels that you can select, depending on the type of features that you want to insert in your page.

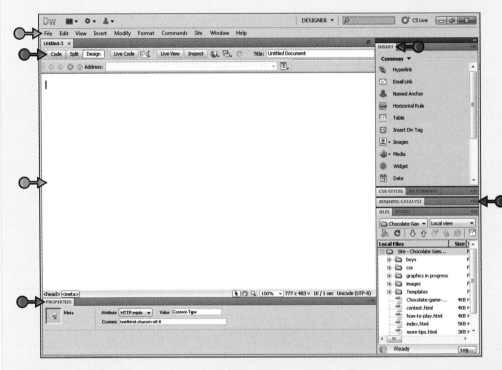

Document window

The main workspace where you insert and arrange the text, images, and other elements of your Web page.

Panels

Can be docked or floated and provide access to many common tools in Dreamweaver, including the Insert, CSS Styles, AP Elements, Business Catalyst, Files, and Assets features.

Properties inspector

Used to display and edit the attributes of any element selected in the Document window.

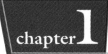
Tour the Dreamweaver Interface on a Macintosh

Dreamweaver CS5 on a Macintosh likewise features
a variety of windows, panels, and inspectors.

Menus

Contain the commands for using
Dreamweaver. Many of these
commands are duplicated within
the windows, panels, and
inspectors of Dreamweaver.

Toolbar

Contains shortcuts to preview and
display features and a text field
where you can specify the title of
a page.

Insert panel

Provides easy access to common
features. There are several different
Insert panels that you can select,
depending on the type of features
that you want to insert in your page.

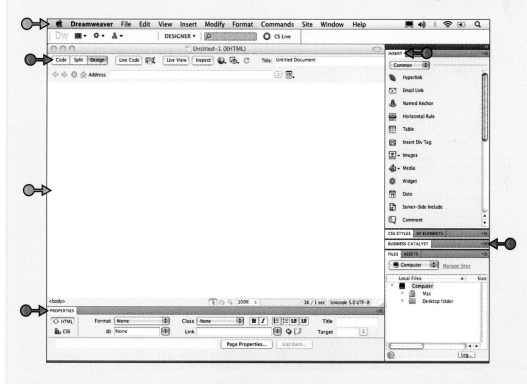

Document window

The main workspace where you
insert and arrange the text,
images, and other elements of
your Web page.

Panels

Can be docked or floated and
provide access to many common
tools in Dreamweaver, including
the Insert, CSS Styles, AP
Elements, Business Catalyst, Files,
and Assets features.

Properties inspector

Used to display and edit the
attributes of any element selected
in the Document window.

You can show or hide accessory windows, also called *panels* and *inspectors*, by using commands on the Window menu. For these and most other features to work in Dreamweaver, you must have a document open in the program. You can create a new document or open any of the files available from the download site that goes with this book, www.DigitalFamily.com/tyv.

Show or Hide a Window

Show a Window

1 Click **Window**.

2 Click the name of the window, panel, or inspector that you want to open.

This example opens the Properties inspector.

● ☑ next to a name indicates that the window, panel, or inspector is open.

● Dreamweaver displays the inspector.

Hide a Window

1 Click **Window**.

2 Click the check-marked (☑) name of the window that you want to hide.

Note: You can click **Window** and then click **Hide Panels** to hide everything except the Document window and toolbar.

Exit Dreamweaver

You can exit Dreamweaver to close the program.

You should always exit Dreamweaver and all other programs before turning off your computer.

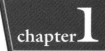

Exit Dreamweaver

1 Click **File**.

2 Click **Exit**.

Before quitting, Dreamweaver alerts you to save any open documents that have unsaved changes.

3 Click **Yes**.

Dreamweaver exits.

Get Help

You can use the help tools that are built into Dreamweaver to find answers to your questions or to learn techniques that you do not know.

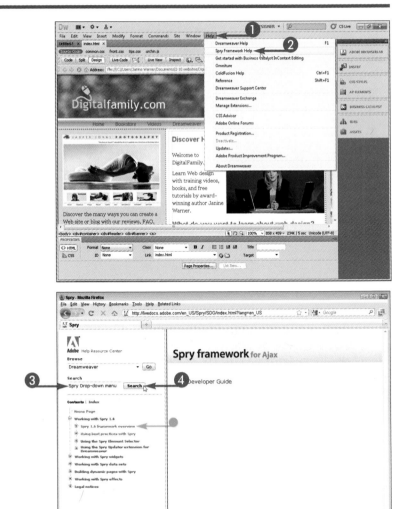

Get Help

1 Click **Help**.

2 Click **Spry Framework Help**.

The Help page opens.

● You can click any topic that you want help with.

3 Type one or more keywords about the topic that you want help with.

Note: You can narrow your search by separating keywords with +.

4 Click **Search**.

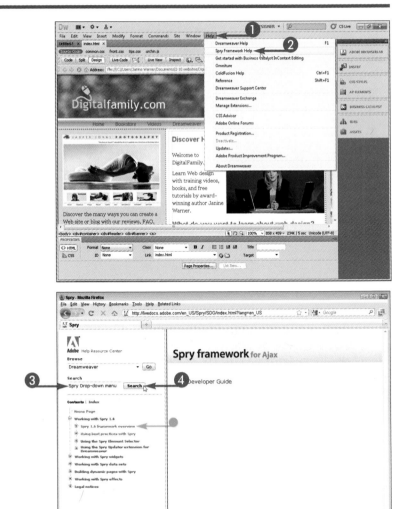

16

A list of topics appears.

⑤ Click a topic from the search result list.

● Information appears on the topic that you selected.

Are there different ways of opening the Help tools and other options in Dreamweaver?

Very often, yes. As with many programs, there is often more than one way to do the same task. For example, you can access many tools and commands, such as Modify Page Properties, by using either a menu or the Properties inspector. You can also use the Split or Code view commands to view and edit the HTML code directly, if you know how to write HTML.

Setting Up Your Web Site

You start a project in Dreamweaver by defining a local root folder where you will store all the files in your Web site on your computer. You can then create your first page and save it in the root folder. This chapter shows you how to set up your Web site.

Define a New Web Site

Before you create your Web pages, you need to define your site in Dreamweaver and set up a root folder where you can store all the files in your site. Defining a root site folder enables Dreamweaver to manage your files in the Files panel and properly set links. As you set up your site, you can create a new folder on your hard drive or select an existing folder as your root folder. For more information on the Files panel, see Chapter 14, "Publishing a Web Site."

Define a New Web Site

1 Click **Site**.

2 Click **New Site**.

The Site Setup dialog box appears.

3 Type a name for your site.

4 Click  to search for your Web site folder.

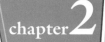

The Choose Root Folder dialog box appears.

⑤ Click here and select the folder that stores your Web pages.

● You can create a new folder for a new site by clicking 🗁, typing in a new name for the folder, and then selecting the new folder.

⑥ Click **Select**.

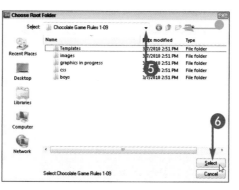

You are returned to the Site Setup dialog box.

⑦ Click **Save**.

If you are setting up an existing site, you will be prompted with a message stating, "The cache will not be re-created." Click **OK**.

Note: Creating a cache enables Dreamweaver to work more efficiently.

● The process can take a few seconds. When complete, the files and folders of the selected site are listed in the Files panel.

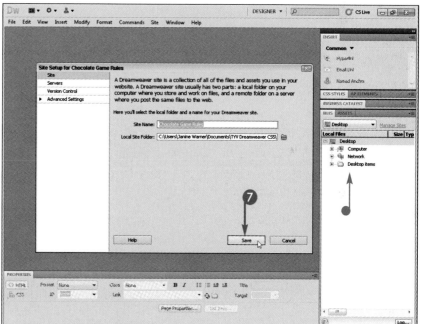

TIP

Why is it important to keep all my Web site files in the same root folder on my computer?

Keeping everything in the same root folder on your local computer enables you to easily transfer your Web site files to a Web server without changing the organization of the files. If your Web site files are not organized on the Web server in the same way that they are organized on your local computer, hyperlinks may not work, and images may not be displayed properly. For more information about working with Web site files and publishing your site to a server, see Chapter 14.

Create a New Web Page

There are multiple ways to create a new page in Dreamweaver CS5. When you launch the program, the initial start page includes useful shortcuts that you can use to create new HTML pages and other kinds of files. When you use the New Document dialog box, covered in this section, you find even more options for the kinds of pages that you can create.

Create a New Web Page

① Click **File**.

② Click **New**.

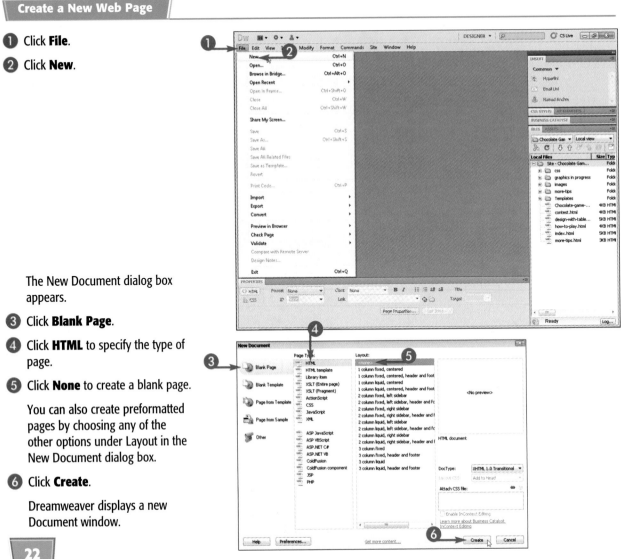

The New Document dialog box appears.

③ Click **Blank Page**.

④ Click **HTML** to specify the type of page.

⑤ Click **None** to create a blank page.

You can also create preformatted pages by choosing any of the other options under Layout in the New Document dialog box.

⑥ Click **Create**.

Dreamweaver displays a new Document window.

Add a Title to a Web Page

A Web page title appears in the title bar when the page opens in a Web browser. The title helps search engines to index pages with more accuracy and is saved in a user's Bookmarks list if he or she bookmarks your Web page.

Add a Title to a Web Page

When you create a new document, an untitled document appears in the main workspace.

Note: *The page name and filename are "Untitled" until you save them.*

1 Type a name for your Web page in the Title text box.

2 Press Enter (Return).

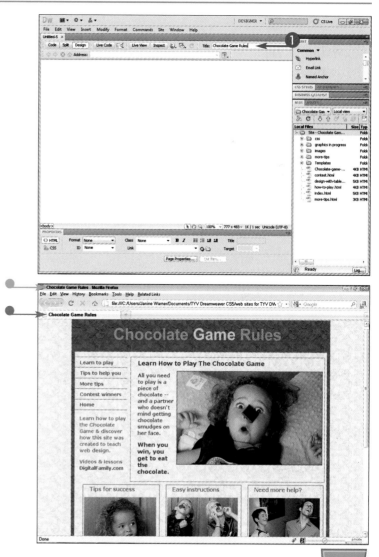

● The Web page title appears in the title bar when the page is displayed in a Web browser.

● If the browser supports tabbed browsing, the title also appears on the tab.

If a visitor to your site bookmarks your page, the title is the text that appears in the Bookmarks list.

Save a Web Page

You should save your Web page as soon as you create it — and again before closing the program or transferring the page to a remote site. It is also a good idea to save all your files frequently to prevent work from being lost due to power outages or system failures. For information about connecting to remote sites, see Chapter 14.

Save a Web Page

Save Your Document

① Click **File**.

② Click **Save**.

● You can click **Save As** to save an existing file with a new filename.

If you are saving a new file for the first time, the Save As dialog box appears.

③ Click here and select your local site folder.

Note: *Your local site folder is where you want to save the pages and other files for your Web site.*

④ Type a name for your Web page.

⑤ Click **Save**.

- Dreamweaver saves the Web page, and the filename and path appear in the title bar.

- You can click ⊠ to close the page.

Revert to an Earlier Version of a Page

1. Click **File**.

2. Click **Revert**.

The page reverts to the previously saved version. All the changes that you made since the last time you saved the file are lost.

Note: If you exit Dreamweaver after you save a document, Dreamweaver cannot revert to the previous version.

Why should I name the main page of my site index.html?

You should name your main Web site or home page index.html because that is the filename that most Web servers open first when a user types a domain name into a Web browser. If you name your main page index.html and it does not open as your first page when your site is on the server, then check with your system administrator or hosting service. Some servers use default.htm or index.htm instead of index.html.

Preview a Web Page in a Browser

You can see how your Web page will appear online by previewing it in a Web browser. The Preview in Browser command works with any Web browser that is installed on your computer. Although Dreamweaver does not ship with Web browser software, Internet Explorer is preinstalled on most computers. Also, you can download Mozilla Firefox for free from www.mozilla.com/firefox.

Preview a Web Page in a Browser

Launch a Web Browser

1. Click the Preview in Browser button ([🌐]).

2. Click a Web browser from the drop-down menu that appears.

   You can also preview the page in your primary Web browser by pressing F12.

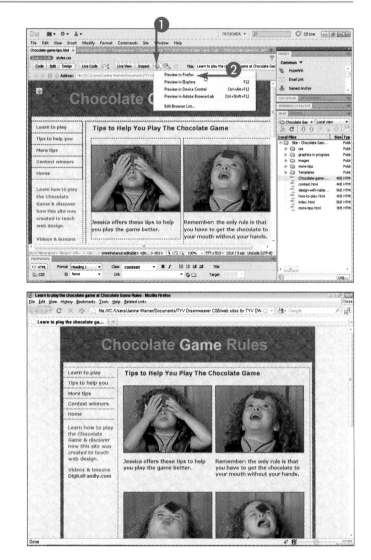

The Web browser launches and opens the current page.

When you preview a Web page in a browser, you can follow links by clicking them, just as you would when viewing Web sites.

Add a Browser

1 Click **File**.

2 Click **Preview in Browser**.

3 Click **Edit Browser List**.

The Preferences dialog box appears.

4 Click ➕.

The Add Browser dialog box appears.

5 Type a name for your Web browser.

6 Click **Browse** and select any Web browser on your computer's hard drive.

7 Click **OK**.

8 Click **OK** to close the Preferences dialog box.

The newly added Web browser will appear in the browser list.

TIP

Why should I use more than one Web browser for previews?

Dreamweaver makes it easy for you to add more than one Web browser because not all Web browsers display Web pages the same way. For example, Internet Explorer and Firefox sometimes display Web pages differently. As a result, it is important to test your pages in a variety of browsers to ensure that they will look good to all your visitors. By using the browser list, you can easily test your Web page in a different Web browser with just a few mouse clicks and adjust your designs until they look good in all the browsers that you think your visitors may use.

3

Exploring the Dreamweaver Interface

In this chapter, you take a tour of the panels and windows that make up the Dreamweaver interface. You will discover all the handy tools and features that make this an award-winning Web design program.

Choose a Workspace Layout

In Dreamweaver CS5, you can choose from several workspace layout options. You can choose from layouts optimized for designers, which focus on the design features of the program, or layouts for coders, which are optimized for those who prefer to work in the code. Choose Classic view if you prefer the way things looked in version CS3.

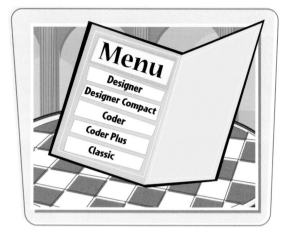

① Click ▼ to select a layout option.

② Click the **Designer Compact** layout option.

The workspace changes to the Designer Compact layout with the panels diminished on the side of the workspace.

③ Click ▼ to select a different layout option.

④ Click the **Coder** layout option.

The workspace changes to the Coder layout, with the Code view open in the workspace.

⑤ Click 🔽 to select a different layout option.

⑥ Click the **Designer** layout option.

The workspace changes to the Designer layout, my personal favorite and the layout option I will use throughout the rest of this book.

TIP

Which layout is right for me?
That depends on the way you work. Dreamweaver CS5 includes many preset workspace layouts. Each is designed to optimize the workspace based on common ways of working in the program. Experiment with the various options, choose the one you like best, and remember that you can click and drag to rearrange the panels and inspectors to change the workspace to best accommodate your preferences.

Customize the Document Window

Dreamweaver CS5 comes with a variety of workspace layouts, and you can customize them further to create an interface that makes your favorite features accessible. You can open and close panels, dock floating features, and save your custom layouts for future use.

Customize the Document Window

① Click **Split**.

The Code view window opens in the left half of the workspace.

② Click ▸▸ to minimize the panels.

The panels are minimized.

● You can click  to expand the panels.

③ Double-click anywhere in the gray bar above the Properties inspector.

The Properties inspector is minimized.

● You can double-click anywhere in the gray bar again to expand the Properties inspector.

TIP

How can I keep my favorite features handy?

You can open or close any of the panels and inspectors in Dreamweaver so that your favorite features are handy when you need them and so that others are out of the way when you do not need them. Most of the panels and other options are available from the Windows menu. For example, to open the CSS Styles panel, you can click **Window** and then click **CSS Styles**. As you work, you may choose to have different panels opened or closed to give you more workspace or to provide easier access to the features that you are using.

Format Content with the Properties Inspector

The Properties inspector enables you to view the properties associated with the object or text that is currently selected in the Document window. Text fields, drop-down menus, buttons, and other form elements in the Properties inspector enable you to modify these properties.

Format an Image

1 Click to select the image.

The image properties appear.

You can change many image properties in the Properties inspector, such as the border size or alignment.

2 To wrap the text around the image, click the **Align** ▾ to open the alignment options.

3 Click an alignment option, such as **Left**.

The text automatically wraps around the image when you apply Left or Right alignment.

4 Create a margin between the image and text by entering the number of pixels of space you want in the **H Space** field.

A margin is created between the image and the text.

Format Text

5 Click and drag to select the text.

6 Click the **Format** ▾.

7 Click to select a heading option, such as **Heading 1**.

Note: The heading tags are an ideal choice for formatting headlines. Heading 1 is the largest, and Heading 6 is the smallest.

● Your text automatically changes to reflect your formatting choices in the Properties inspector.

You can change many text properties in the Properties inspector.

● The Properties inspector includes HTML and CSS options.

Note: For many formatting choices, such as font and size, you must create styles. You can find instructions for creating styles using cascading style sheets in Chapter 12, "Creating and Applying Cascading Style Sheets."

TIP

When would I use more than one font on a Web page?

When you choose a font face in Dreamweaver, the program offers fonts in groups of three. For example, one option is Arial, Helvetica, and sans-serif, and another option is Times New Roman, Times, and serif. Dreamweaver provides these collections because the fonts that are displayed on a Web page are determined by the available fonts on the visitor's computer. Because you cannot guarantee what fonts a user will have, Web browsers use the first font that matches in a list of fonts. Thus, in the first example, the font will be displayed as follows: in Arial if the Arial font is on the visitor's computer; in Helvetica if Arial is not available; and in any available sans-serif font if neither of the first two fonts is available.

Open a Panel

Dreamweaver features a highly customizable workspace. You can move panels around the screen by clicking the top bar of a panel and dragging. All the panels can float or lock into place at the side of the program. You can open or close and expand or collapse panels. To find additional panel options, click the tabs at the top of each panel.

Open a Panel

① Click **Window**.

② Click the name of the panel that you want to open, such as **Files**.

● The panel appears; in the example of the Files panel, it displays all the files in the Web site.

③ Click a tab to open a related panel, such as the **Assets** panel.

The panel appears.

● In the Assets panel, you can click any of the buttons to display the assets that it represents, such as the Images button (⬛).

④ Click ⬛.

● All the available images in the site appear in the Assets panel.

⑤ Click any image filename to preview the image in the display area at the top of the Assets panel.

⑥ Double-click anywhere in the gray bar at the top of the Files panel to close the panel.

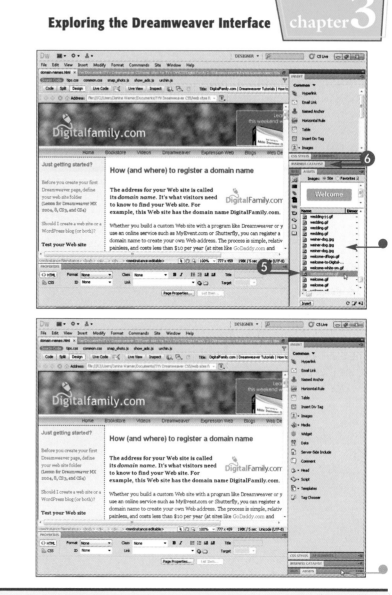

In this example, the Files and Assets panels collapse.

Note: *When you collapse a panel such as the Files panel, other panels become more visible.*

● You can double-click the gray bar on any panel to open it and then click any tab in an open panel to make it active.

How can I keep track of my assets?
The Assets panel provides access to many handy features, such as the Colors assets, which list all the colors that are used on a site. For example, this is useful if you are using a particular text color and you want to use the same color consistently on every page. Similarly, the Links assets make it easy to access links that are used elsewhere in your site so that you can quickly and easily set frequently used links.

Open and Customize the Insert Panel

You can insert elements, such as images, tables, and layers, into your pages with the Insert panel. Located at the top of the window, the panel features a drop-down menu that reveals options such as Common elements, Forms, and Text.

Open and Customize the Insert Panel

1 Click **Window**.

2 Click **Insert**.

● The Insert panel appears.

3 Click here.

4 Click **Hide Labels**.

● The labels are no longer visible, and the icons are rearranged to take up less space.

⑤ Click the gray bar above any panel and drag it to enlarge or reduce the size.

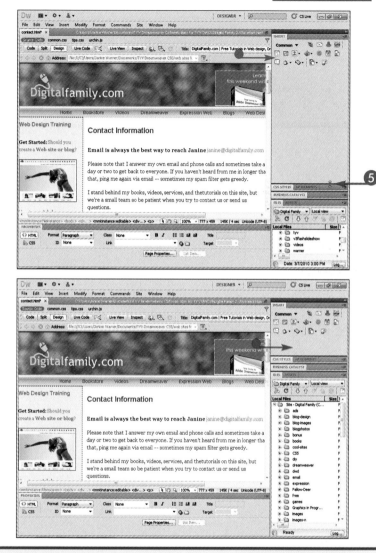

● The panel adjusts to fill the space based on where you dragged it.

Note: *You can adjust the panels as much or as little as you like.*

How can I save the workspace once I get it the way I want it?

After you have all the panels and inspectors the way that you want them in Dreamweaver, you can save the entire workspace as a custom layout. Click **Window ➪ Workspace Layout ➪ New Workspace**. In the New Workspace dialog box, give the layout a name. Then you can select the custom layout just as you would select any other workspace layout.

Set Preferences

You can easily change many options in Dreamweaver by changing the settings in the Preferences dialog box. This enables you to modify the interface and many default options to customize Dreamweaver to better suit how you like to work.

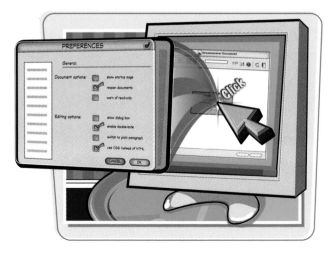

1 Click **Edit**.

2 Click **Preferences**.

The Preferences dialog box appears.

3 Click a Preferences category.

In this example, the Status Bar category is selected.

● Options appear for the category that you selected.

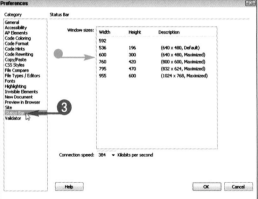

④ Change the settings for the property that you want to alter.

● In this example, the Connection Speed option is set to 128Kb.

⑤ Click **OK**.

The changes take effect immediately.

● In this example, the status bar now displays download times that assume a 128Kb connection speed.

How do I ensure that Dreamweaver does not change my HTML or other code?

You can select options under the Code Rewriting category in the Preferences dialog box to ensure that Dreamweaver does not automatically correct or modify your code. For example, you can turn off the error-correcting functions, specify the files that Dreamweaver should not rewrite based on file extension, and disable the character-encoding features.

Working with XHTML

Dreamweaver helps you to build Web pages by automatically writing the XHTML code as you create pages in Design view. This chapter introduces the code behind your pages, as well as the tools in Dreamweaver that enable you to edit XHTML code.

Introducing XHTML

Although Dreamweaver writes the XHTML code for you, which can save you time and trouble, learning the basics of XHTML can help you better understand how Web design works. And you always have the option of writing or editing the code manually.

XHTML

Extensible hypertext markup language (XHTML) is the formatting language that you can use to create Web pages. When you open a Web page in a Web browser, the XHTML code tells the Web browser how to display the text, images, and other content on the page. By default, Dreamweaver CS5 writes XHTML Transitional instead of HTML because XHTML is a stricter version of HTML that is designed to comply with contemporary Web standards.

XHTML Tags

The basic unit of XHTML is called a *tag.* You can recognize XHTML tags by their angle brackets:

```
<h1>This is a headline</h1>

<p>It is followed by some plain
text in a paragraph tag. <b>This
text will appear bold because it
is surrounded by the bold tag.</b>
This text will not be bold.</p>
```

You can format text and other elements on your page by placing them inside the XHTML tags. When you use the formatting tools in Dreamweaver, the program automatically inserts tags in the code.

How Tags Work

Some XHTML tags work in pairs. Open and close tags surround content in a document and control the formatting of the content, such as when the `<strong>` and `</strong>` tags set off bold text. Other tags can stand alone, such as the `<br />` tag, which adds a line break. XHTML tags must have a closing tag, even if there is only one tag, and close tags always contain a forward slash (/). This is why the line break tag in XHTML looks like this: `<br />`. XHTML must be written in lowercase letters.

Create Web Pages without Knowing XHTML

Dreamweaver streamlines the process of creating Web pages by giving you an easy-to-use, visual interface with which you can generate XHTML code. You specify formatting with menu commands and button clicks, and Dreamweaver takes care of writing the underlying XHTML code. When you build a Web page in the Document window, you can see your page as it will appear in a Web browser instead of as XHTML code.

Edit XHTML Documents in a Text Editor

Because XHTML documents are plain-text files, you can open and edit them with any text editor. In fact, in the early days of the Web, most people created their pages with simple editors such as Notepad (in Windows) and SimpleText (for the Macintosh). If you use Dreamweaver, you have the advantage of being able to write XHTML code when you want to or letting Dreamweaver write it for you.

Direct Access to the XHTML Code

Dreamweaver allows you direct access to the raw XHTML code. This is helpful if you want to edit the code directly. In Dreamweaver, you can work in Code view, Design view, or Split view, which enables you to see the Code and Design views simultaneously. You can also use the Quick Tag Editor to edit code without switching to Code or Design view.

Work in Design View and Code View

You can switch to Code view in the Document window to inspect and edit the XHTML and other code on the Web page. You can use the Split view to see both the XHTML code and Design view at the same time.

You will probably do most of your work in Design view, which displays your page the way it will appear in most Web browsers, but it is a good practice to use Split view because it can help you learn XHTML.

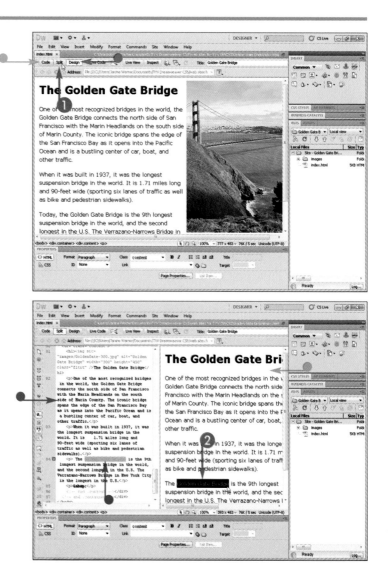

Work in Design View and Code View

1. In the Document window, click the **Split** view button.

● You can click the **Code** view button to display the source code of your page in the Document window.

● You can click the **Design** view button to hide the code and view only the page design as it would appear in a Web browser.

Both Code view and Design view appear in the Document window when you click **Split**.

● The XHTML and other code appear in the left pane.

● The Design view appears in the right pane.

2. Click and drag to select some text in the Design view pane.

● The corresponding code becomes highlighted in the Code view pane.

③ Type to edit the text in the Code view pane.

● The corresponding text is automatically updated in the Design view pane.

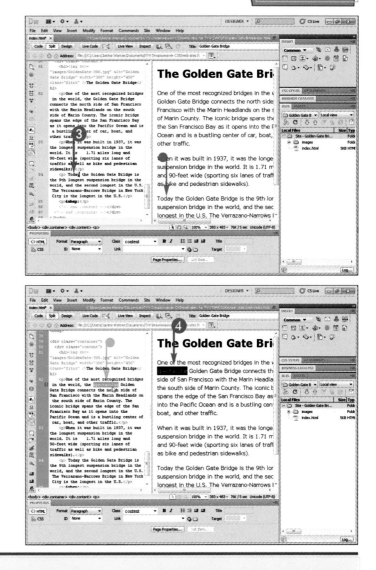

④ Click in the Design view pane and type to make changes.

● The content in the Code view pane is updated as you make your changes.

TIP

How do I change Split view to horizontal instead of vertical?

In Dreamweaver CS5, the default Split view is split with the code on the left and the design on the right, when you choose the Split workspace layout. You can change the Code view to horizontal (as it was in the previous versions CS4 and CS3) by choosing **View ➪ Split Vertically** to deselect this option.

Explore Head and Body Tags

Every XHTML document contains head and body tags. To view the XHTML code of a Web page, you can click the Code view button in the Document window, or you can click **Window** and then click **Code Inspector**.

DOCTYPE

The DOCTYPE describes the document and identifies that it was created with XHTML 1.0 Transitional, which is currently recommended for most Web pages.

<html> tags

Open and close <html> tags begin and end every HTML document.

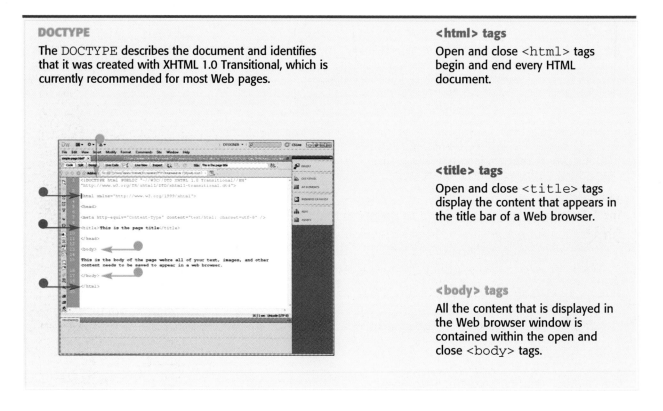

<title> tags

Open and close <title> tags display the content that appears in the title bar of a Web browser.

<body> tags

All the content that is displayed in the Web browser window is contained within the open and close <body> tags.

Explore Block-Formatting Tags

XHTML is made up of many different tags, each designed to specify a particular kind of formatting, such as paragraph breaks, headline styles, and bulleted lists. The same page is displayed in these two figures, first in Code view and then in Design view.

Code View

This page is displayed in Code view in Dreamweaver.

<div> tag

The <div> tag is used to divide content and is often combined with styles that are created in CSS.

<h1> to <h6> tags

The heading tags are ideal for formatting headlines. The <h1> tag creates the largest heading style, whereas the <h6> tag is the smallest.

<img src> tag

The <img src> tag is used to insert an image into a page.

<p> tags

The open and close <p> tags separate paragraphs of content and add a space between images and other elements.

Design View

This is the same page displayed in Design view.

<div> tag

The <div> tag is displayed in Design view as a box. The width and centering of the container is defined with a CSS style.

<h1> to <h6> tags

The <h1> tag makes the headline text large and bold.

<p> tags

The <p> tag separates content into paragraph blocks and adds space around images and other elements.

<img src> tag

The <img src> tag displays the image on the page.

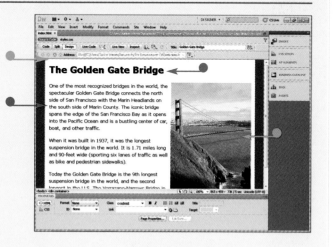

Clean Up HTML Code

Dreamweaver can optimize the code in your Web pages by deleting redundant or nonfunctional tags. This can decrease the page file size and make the source code easier to read in Code view.

It is easy to create unused tags when you do things such as copy and paste content. To keep formatting more consistent, it is a good idea to delete unused tags by running the Clean Up XHTML command.

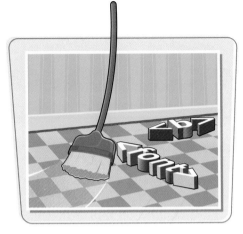

Clean Up HTML Code

① Click **Split** to display the Code view and Design view at the same time.

● In this example, there are two empty <h1> tags.

● The extra <h1> tags add blank space to the top of the page.

② Click **Commands**.

③ Click **Clean Up XHTML**.

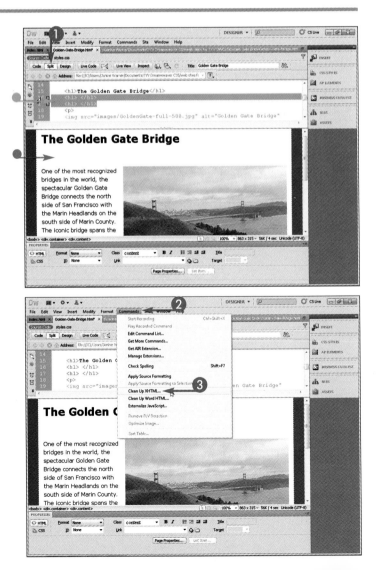

The Clean Up HTML/XHTML dialog box appears.

④ Click the options for code that you want to remove or clean up (☐ changes to ☑).

⑤ Click **OK**.

● Dreamweaver parses the HTML code and displays the results, including a summary of what was removed.

⑥ Click **OK**.

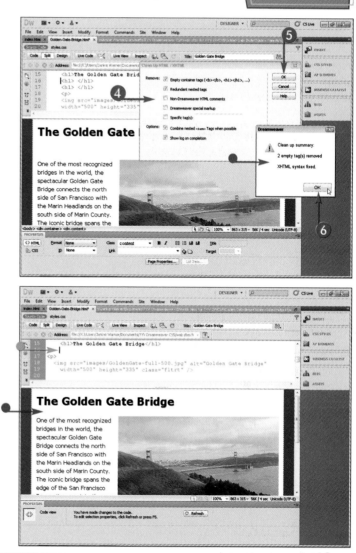

● The cleaned-up HTML code appears in the Document window. In this example, the two empty <h1> tags were removed.

● The corresponding changes are also visible in Design view. In this example, there is no longer any extra space at the top of the page.

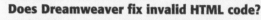

TIPS

How do empty tags end up appearing in the Dreamweaver HTML code?

Sometimes when you edit text in the Document window, for example, by cutting and pasting sentences and reformatting words, Dreamweaver removes text from within tags without removing the actual tags, leaving the formatting code behind.

Does Dreamweaver fix invalid HTML code?

By default, Dreamweaver rewrites some instances of invalid HTML code. When you open an HTML document, Dreamweaver rewrites tags that are not nested properly, closes tags that are not allowed to remain open, and removes extra closing tags. If Dreamweaver does not recognize a tag, it highlights it in red and displays it in the Document window, but it does not remove the tag. You can change or turn off this behavior by clicking **Edit**, then clicking **Preferences**, and then selecting the category **Code Rewriting**.

View and Edit Head Content

Dreamweaver gives you various ways to view, add to, and edit the head content of a Web page. For example, meta tags store special descriptive information about the page that can be used by search engines.

View and Edit Head Content

Insert Meta Keywords

1. Click **Insert**.

2. Click **HTML**.

3. Click **Head Tags**.

4. Click **Keywords**.

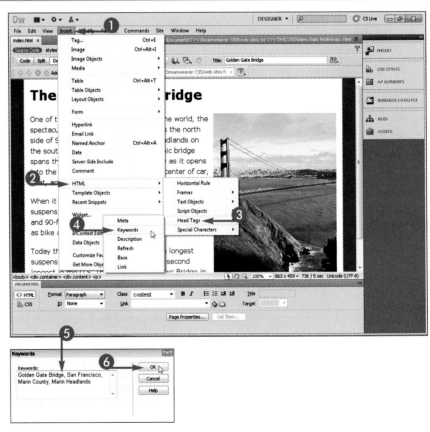

The Keywords dialog box appears.

5. Type a series of keywords, separated by commas, that describe the content of the page.

6. Click **OK**.

The keywords are added to the code.

Note: *Keywords are not displayed in Design view or in a Web browser.*

Insert a Meta Description

1. Click **Insert**.
2. Click **HTML**.
3. Click **Head Tags**.
4. Click **Description**.

The Description dialog box appears.

5. Type a brief description of the content of the page.

6. Click **OK**.

The description is added to the code.

Note: Descriptions are not displayed in Design view or in a Web browser.

How can I influence how search engines rank my pages?

Some search engines give greater importance to the description and keyword information that you add to the head content of HTML documents than others, but it is always a good practice to include it. You can also improve search engine ranking by including keywords in the title tag of the page.

Make Quick Edits to XHTML Tags

You can get quick access to XHTML and other code by using the Quick Tag Editor. The Quick Tag Editor is a handy way to make quick changes to tags without using Code view.

Make Quick Edits to XHTML Tags

Use the Quick Tag Editor

1 Click to place your cursor in an area of the page that you want to edit, such as this headline.

Note: It is not necessary to select the entire text section or image to select the tag.

2 Right-click (**Control** + click) the tag that you want to edit in the Tag selector.

3 Click **Quick Tag Editor**.

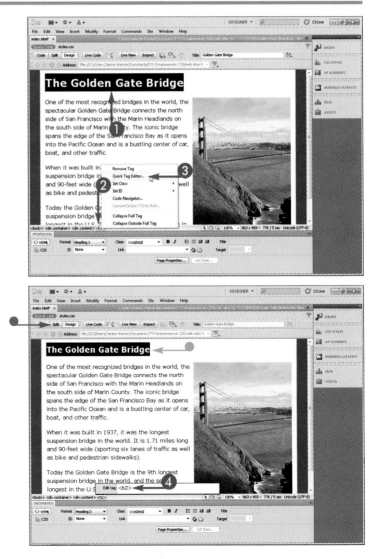

4 Click to select the tag and type to replace, delete, or add more text.

5 Press **Enter** (**Return**).

● The tag is automatically changed in the HTML code, and the change becomes visible in the Tag selector and in the formatting in Design view.

● You can click **Split** to view the code if you want to check your work.

Remove a Tag

1. Click to place your cursor in an area of the page that you want to edit, such as this bold text formatted with the `<strong>` tag.

Note: It is not necessary to select the entire text section or image to select the tag.

2. Right-click (Control + click) the tag that you want to remove in the Tag selector.

3. Click **Remove Tag**.

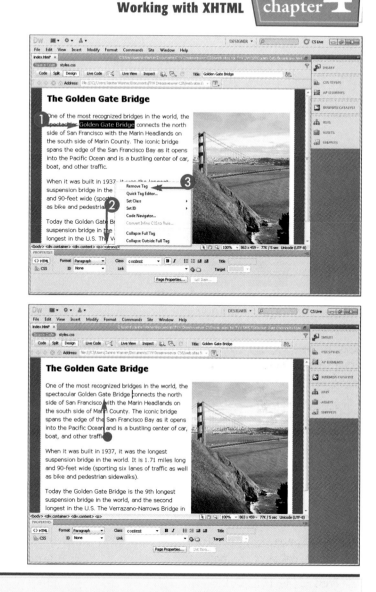

● The tag and any related formatting is removed. In this example, the text is no longer bold.

Note: When you want to change the way text or other content is formatted, removing a tag before adding more formatting is a good practice because it can prevent multiple tags from being applied to the same content.

TIPS

Does Dreamweaver support all XHTML tags?

Dreamweaver CS5 includes the vast majority of XHTML tags in its many menus and panels. You can also write your own tags in Code view if you want to use tags that are not supported in Dreamweaver's features. When you write XHTML in Code view, Dreamweaver automatically provides assistance with its code completion features.

What does the text Lorem ipsum dolor mean that appears in Web templates?

The text is Latin, a commonly used language for "dummy" text that is used as a placeholder when laying out pages. Although Latin text is often used as placeholder text in designs, its meaning generally has nothing to do with its usage. The idea is that using Latin text will make it obvious that the text still needs to be replaced.

Using Code Snippets to Add Special Formatting

You can insert short pieces of prewritten code from the Snippets panel. This is a handy feature for adding special formatting and for storing commonly used formatting options where they are easy to apply to the page.

Using Code Snippets to Add Special Formatting

① Click **Window**.

② Click **Snippets**.

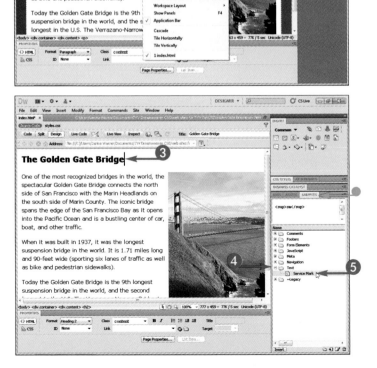

● The Snippets panel appears.

③ Click to place your cursor where you want the snippet to appear in your page.

④ Click + to open a snippet collection.

⑤ Double-click a snippet to insert it.

- The snippet is inserted into the document.

6 Double-click the gray bar at the top of the panel group to close the Snippets panel.

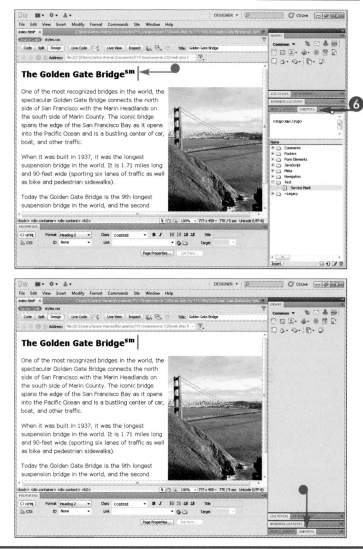

- The panel group closes.

How many snippets can I use?

You can choose from a variety of snippets included with Dreamweaver, and you can create your own to make it easy to add frequently used pieces of code to your pages.

Formatting and Styling Text

Text is the easiest type of information to add to a Web page using Dreamweaver. This chapter shows you how to create and format headlines, paragraphs, bulleted lists, and stylized text.

Create a Heading

When you format text with heading tags, you can create large, bold text and specify a range of sizes. Heading 1 is the largest, and Heading 6 is the smallest.

Create a Heading

① Click and drag to select the text that you want to use for a main heading.

② Click the **Format** ▼.

③ Click **Heading 1**.

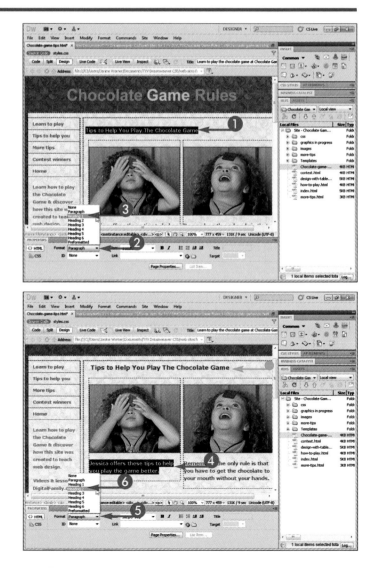

● The font size changes to the largest heading size, and the text changes to bold. White space separates it from other text.

④ Click and drag to select text that you want to use for a second-level heading.

⑤ Click the **Format** ▼.

⑥ Click **Heading 2**.

● The text changes to second-level headline, with a size slightly smaller than the first, and it also becomes bold.

Note: The higher the heading number, the smaller the text formatting.

⑦ Click and drag to select text that you want to use for a third-level heading.

⑧ Click the **Format** ☐.

⑨ Click **Heading 3**.

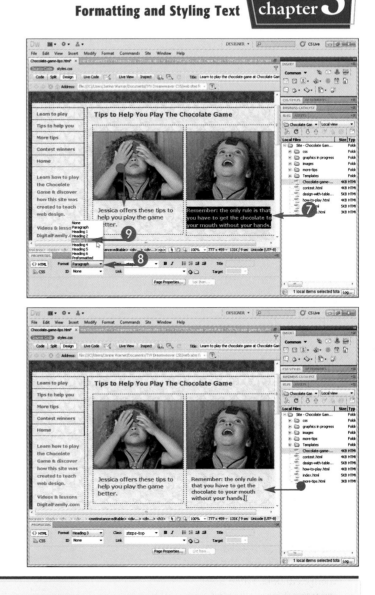

● The headline changes to a size smaller than the Heading 2 size but remains bold.

Note: Using cascading style sheets, covered in Chapter 12, "Creating and Applying Cascading Style Sheets," you can change the appearance of text formatted with the heading tags.

TIPS

What heading levels should I use to format my text?

Headings 1, 2, and 3 are often used for titles and subtitles. Heading 4 is similar to a bold version of default text. Headings 5 and 6 are often used for smaller text, such as copyright or disclaimer information.

Why are my headlines different sizes when I see them on another computer?

Size can vary from one computer to the next, and some users set their Web browsers to display larger or smaller type on their computers. Browsers use the default text size to determine the size of the heading. For example, Heading 1 text is three times larger than the default text size, and Heading 6 text is one-third the default size.

Create Paragraphs

You can organize the text on your Web page by creating and aligning paragraphs. When you press Enter (or Return for a Mac), you add a paragraph tag to the code, which creates a line break and space between paragraphs.

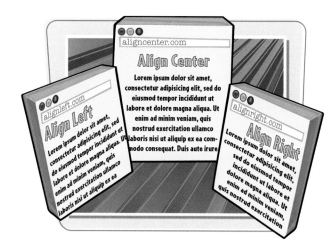

① Type the text for your Web page in the Document window.

② Position the cursor where you want a paragraph break.

③ Press Enter (Return).

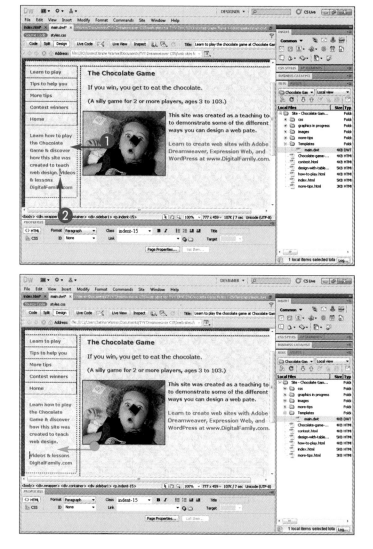

● A blank line appears between the blocks of text, separating the text into paragraphs.

Note: Paragraphs align left by default.

④ Click and drag to select the paragraph that you want to align.

⑤ Click **Format**.

⑥ Click **Align**.

⑦ Choose an alignment option to align your paragraph.

● The paragraph aligns on the page.

Note: You can also control the alignment of text, images, and other content using cascading style sheets, covered in Chapter 12.

TIPS

What controls the width of the paragraphs on my Web page?

The width of your paragraphs depends on the width of the Web browser window or the container that surrounds your text. You can use tables or `div` tags with CSS to control the width of your paragraphs. If you do not, when a user changes the size of the browser window, the widths of the paragraphs will also change. For more information on tables, see Chapter 8. For more information on CSS, see Chapters 12 and 13.

What is the HTML code for paragraphs?

In HTML, paragraphs are surrounded by opening `<p>` and closing `</p>` tags. You can click the **Code** view button to view the HTML code of the page.

Create Line Breaks

When you do not want a full paragraph break, you can use line breaks to keep lines of text adjacent. When you hold down the Shift key and press Enter (or the Shift key and Return for a Mac), you create a line break.

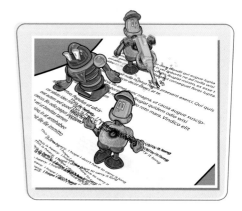

Create Line Breaks

1 Click where you want the line of text to break.

2 Press Shift + Enter (Return).

● Dreamweaver adds a line break.

Note: You can combine paragraph and line breaks to add more space between lines of text.

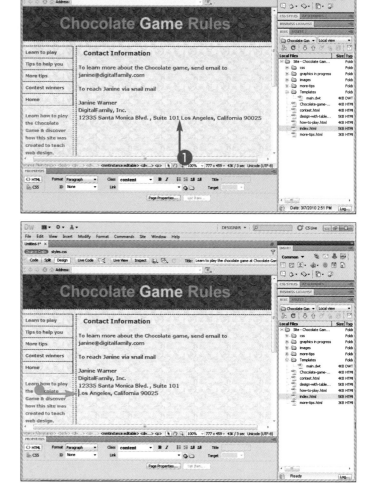

Indent Paragraphs with Blockquote

HTML includes a tag called `<blockquote>`, which is commonly used to indent paragraphs of text. Technically, this tag should be reserved for long quotes, but you can use it to make selected paragraphs stand out from the rest of the text on your Web page in much the same way you would use the indent feature in a word-processing program.

Indent Paragraphs with Blockquote

1 Click and drag to select a paragraph or series of paragraphs.

2 Click ▤ to indent the text.

● Additional space appears in both the left and right margins of the paragraph.

You can repeat steps **1** and **2** to indent the paragraph further.

● You can outdent an indented paragraph by clicking ▤.

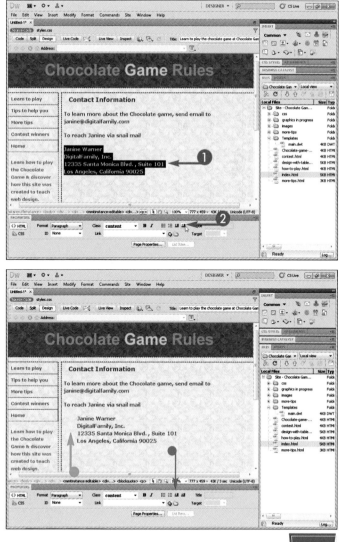

You can organize text items into ordered and unordered lists. Unordered lists have items that are indented and bulleted. Ordered lists have items that are indented and numbered or lettered.

Create Lists

Create an Unordered List

1. Type your list items in the Document window.

2. Click between the items and press Enter (Return) to place each item in a separate paragraph.

3. Click and drag to select all the list items.

4. Click the Unordered List button (≡) in the Properties inspector.

● The list items appear indented and bulleted.

Create an Ordered List

1. Type your list items in the Document window.

2. Click between the items and press Enter (Return) to place each item in a separate paragraph.

3. Click and drag to select all the list items.

4. Click the Ordered List button (⊞) in the Properties inspector.

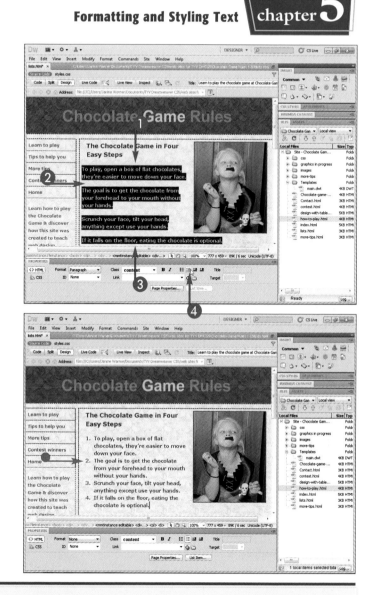

● The list items appear indented and numbered.

Can I modify the appearance of my unordered list?

Yes. You can modify the style of an unordered list by highlighting an item in the list and clicking **Format**, then clicking **List**, and then clicking **Properties**. The dialog box that appears enables you to select different bullet styles for your unordered list.

Can I modify the appearance of my ordered list with CSS?

Yes. You can create CSS style rules for the ul, ol, and li tags and change the spacing, alignment, and other formatting elements of lists. You can find instructions for creating CSS styles in Chapter 12.

Insert Common Special Characters

You can insert special characters into your Web page that do not appear on your keyboard, such as the copyright symbol, trademark symbol, and letters with accent marks.

Insert Common Special Characters

① Click where you want to insert the special character.

② Click **Insert**.

③ Click **HTML**.

④ Click **Special Characters**.

⑤ Click the special character that you want to insert.

● The special character appears in your Web page text.

The HTML code that defines that special character is inserted into the HTML code of the page.

● You can add space, edit, and format special characters as you would any other text on your Web page.

Why do special characters look strange in my Web browser?
Although most Web browsers display double quotation marks without problems, some standard punctuation marks are considered special characters and require special code. If you do not use the special HTML code, those characters may not be displayed properly.

Insert Other Special Characters

You can add many more special characters, such as accent marks and other language symbols, into your Web page by using the Other option in the Special Characters list.

Insert Other Special Characters

① Click where you want to insert the special character.

② Click **Insert**.

③ Click **HTML**.

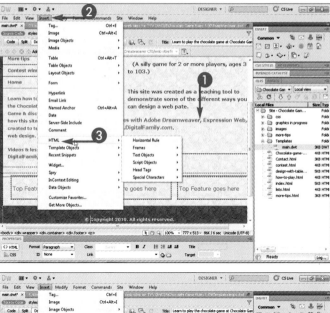

④ Click **Special Characters**.

⑤ Click **Other**.

The Insert Other Character dialog box appears, displaying a wider variety of special characters.

⑥ Click a special character.

⑦ Click **OK**.

● The special character appears in your Web page.

The HTML code that defines that special character is inserted into the HTML code of the page.

TIP

How do I include non-English-language text on my Web page?

Many foreign languages feature accented characters that do not appear on standard keyboards. You can insert most of these characters using the Special Characters feature described here.

Hola amigos virtuales,

Me encanta viajar a América Latina y España.

Copy Text from Another Document

You can save time by copying and pasting text from an existing document, instead of typing it all over again. This is particularly convenient when you have a lot of text in a word-processing program such as Microsoft Word or data in a spreadsheet in a program such as Excel. When you paste text in Dreamweaver, you have multiple formatting choices.

Copy Text from Another Document

① Click and drag to select text in the original file, such as this document created in Microsoft Word.

② Click the Copy button.

Alternatively, you can use
Ctrl + C (⌘ + C).

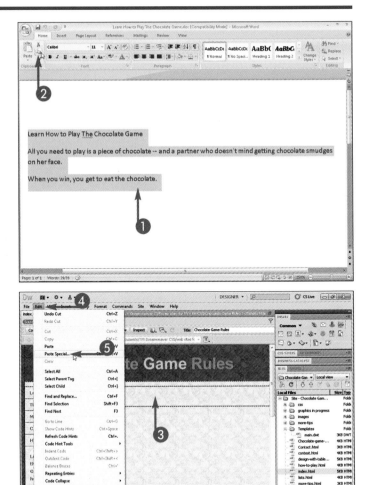

③ Click where you want to insert the text.

④ Click **Edit**.

⑤ Click **Paste Special**.

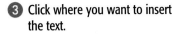

The Paste Special dialog box opens.

6 Click a Paste option.

7 Click **OK**.

● The text is inserted into the HTML file.

Dreamweaver automatically formats the text in HTML, based on the formatting option that you selected in the Paste Special dialog box.

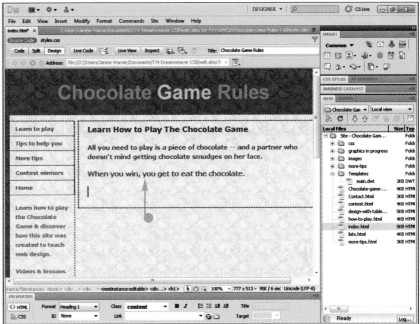

When is it a good idea to copy and paste text?

Even if you type at speeds of over 100 words per minute, you can save time if you do not have to retype all your documents. If your original text file was created using a word-processing program such as Microsoft Word, you can speed up the process by importing the Word document into Dreamweaver. You can also copy and paste text from Excel documents, and Dreamweaver automatically builds tables to duplicate the formatting from Excel. After you have pasted the content into Dreamweaver, you can edit and format the text or other data as you normally would.

Working with Images and Multimedia

Make your Web page more interesting by adding photos, graphics, animation, video, and other visual elements. This chapter shows you how to insert and format these elements. To help you follow along, you can download the entire Web site and all the images, videos, and other files featured in this chapter from the author's site at www.DigitalFamily.com/tyv.

Insert an Image into a Web Page

You can insert different types of images into your Web page, including clip art, digital camera images, and scanned photos. You must first save the images in a Web format, such as GIF, PNG, or JPEG.

Insert an Image into a Web Page

1 Click to position ▷ where you want to insert the image.

2 Click **Insert**.

3 Click **Image**.

● You can also click the Images button (▣) in the Common Insert panel.

The Select Image Source dialog box appears.

4 Click ▾ and select the folder that contains the image.

5 Click the image file that you want to insert into your Web page.

● A preview of the image appears.

● You can insert an image that exists at an external Web address by typing the address into the **URL** field.

6 Click **OK**.

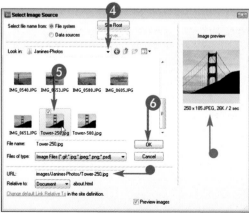

The Image Tag Accessibility Attributes dialog box appears.

⑦ Enter a description of the image.

Note: Alternate text is displayed only if the image is not visible. It is important for visually impaired visitors who use screen readers to "read" Web pages to them.

⑧ Enter a URL for a longer description, if available.

⑨ Click **OK**.

● The image appears where you positioned your cursor in the Web page.

To delete an image, click the image and press Del.

Wrap Text around an Image

You can wrap text around an image by aligning the image to one side of a Web page. Wrapping text around images enables you to fit more information onto the screen and gives your Web pages a more finished, professional look. There are many alignment options. Experiment to find the best effect for your page.

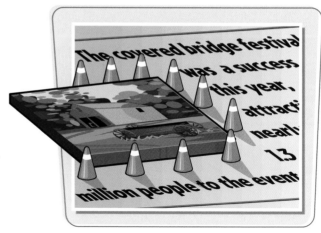

Align an Image

① Click the image to select it.

② Click the **Align** ▼.

③ Click an alignment option to position the image.

● You can click here to expand the Properties inspector if the alignment options are not visible.

● The text flows around the image according to the alignment that you selected.

In this example, the text flows to the right of the left-aligned image.

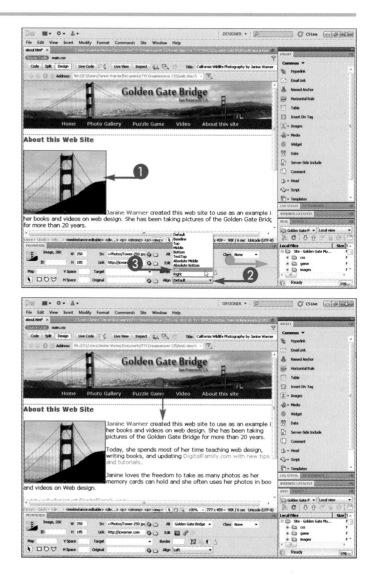

● You can select other options from the **Align** menu for different wrapping effects, such as **Right** or **Middle**.

● In this example, the text flows to the left of the right-aligned image.

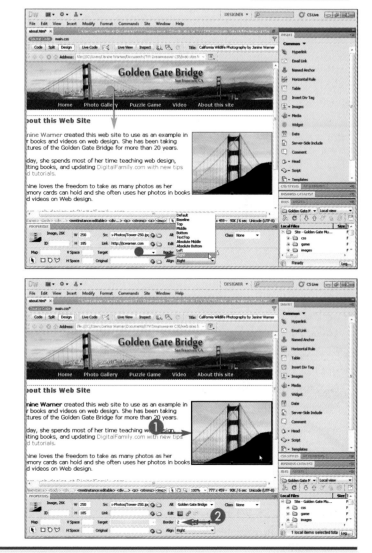

Add a Border to an Image

① Click the image to select it.

② Type a width into the **Border** field.

This example uses a border of 2 pixels.

A black border appears around the image. If the image is a link, the border appears in the link color.

Note: To learn how to change link colors, see Chapter 7, "Creating Hyperlinks."

How can I determine the download time for my Web page?

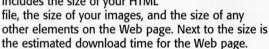

The total size of your Web page appears in kilobytes (KB) on the status bar at the bottom of the workspace. The total size includes the size of your HTML file, the size of your images, and the size of any other elements on the Web page. Next to the size is the estimated download time for the Web page.

What is the ideal size of a Web page?

Most Web designers feel comfortable putting up a page with a total size under 150KB. However, there are exceptions to this rule. For example, you may want to break this rule for an especially important image file. The 150KB limit does not apply to multimedia files, although multimedia files should be kept as small as possible.

Add Space around an Image

You can add space around an image to create a margin and separate the image from any text or other images on your Web page. This creates a cleaner page layout and makes it easier to read the text that wraps around an image.

Add Space to the Left and Right of an Image

1 Click the image to select it.

2 Type an amount in the **H Space** field.

Note: H space is measured in pixels.

3 Press Enter (Return).

● Extra space appears to the left and right of the image.

Add Space Above and Below an Image

1 Click the image to select it.

2 Type an amount in pixels in the **V Space** field.

3 Press Enter (Return).

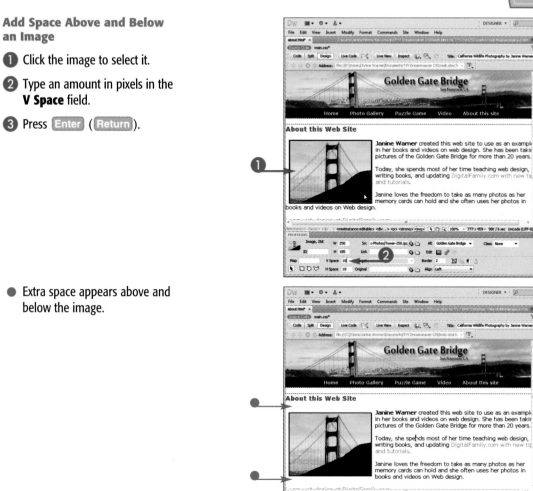

● Extra space appears above and below the image.

Is there a more precise way to add space around my image?

In many cases, adding space around your images enhances the appearance of your Web page. The extra space makes text easier to read and keeps adjacent images from appearing as a single image. However, when you add space using the horizontal and vertical space options in Dreamweaver, you add space to all sides of the image. If you want to create space only on one side, you can create a style using CSS margin settings to add space to just that side. You learn more about CSS in Chapters 12 and 13.

Crop an Image

You can trim, or *crop*, an image by using the Crop tool and dragging the crop handles to adjust how much of the image you want to delete. This can be useful for quick edits without using an external image-editing program, as it physically crops the image file.

Crop an Image

① Click the image to select it.

② Click the Crop tool button (📷).

A dialog box appears.

● You can turn off this warning by clicking the check box (☐ changes to ☑).

③ Click **OK**.

④ Click and drag the black square handles to define the area that you want to crop.

The part of the photo that appears grayed out will be deleted.

⑤ Double-click inside the crop box.

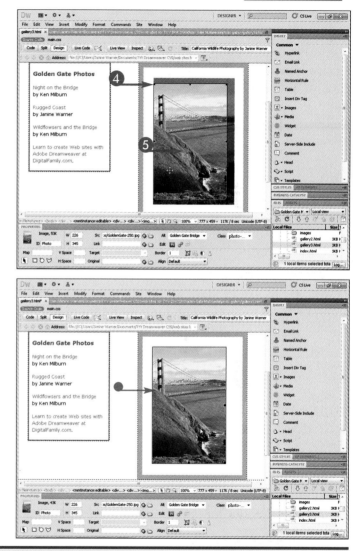

● The image is trimmed to the size of the crop box.

Note: Keep in mind that when you save the page, the image is permanently cropped.

TIP

Should I edit images in Dreamweaver or use an external graphics program?

Adobe has added the Crop and other basic editing tools to make working on a Web page faster and easier. If you need to do a simple crop, the Crop tool is faster than opening the image in an image-editing program such as Adobe Fireworks or Adobe Photoshop. However, if you want to save a copy of the original before you make the crop or do other image editing, then you need to use a dedicated image-editing program.

Resize an Image

You can change the display size of an image without changing the file size of the image. You can do this by changing the pixel size or by clicking and dragging the corner of the image.

Pixels are tiny, solid-color squares that make up a digital image. When you specify a size in pixels, you are using a very small unit of measurement.

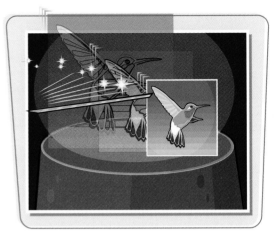

Resize an Image

Resize Using Pixel Dimensions

1 Click the image to select it.

● The dimensions of the image appear.

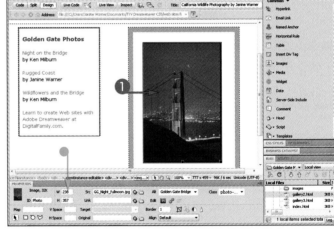

2 Type the width that you want in pixels.

3 Press Enter (Return).

4 Type the height that you want in pixels.

5 Press Enter (Return).

● The image is displayed with its new dimensions.

Click and Drag to Resize

① Click the image to select it.

② Drag one of the handles at the edge of the image ($\llcorner$ changes to $\llcorner_\searrow$).

To resize the image proportionally, press and hold down **Shift** as you drag a corner.

The image expands or contracts to the new size.

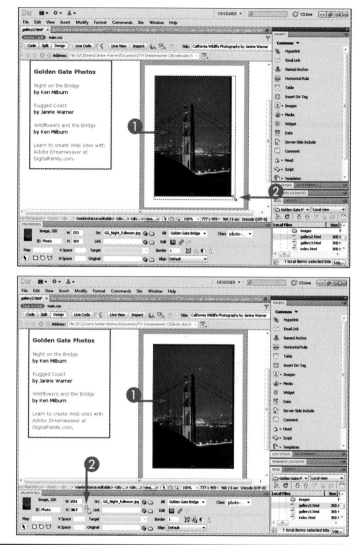

Reset the Image to Its Original Size

Note: *You can reset any image to its original size.*

① Click the image to select it.

② Click the Reset Size button (⟳) in the Properties inspector.

The image returns to its original size.

TIP

What is the best way to change the dimensions of an image on a Web page?

Although you can quickly change the display size of an image by changing the pixel dimensions in the Properties inspector or by clicking and dragging to stretch or shrink it on the Web page, this does not actually resize the image's true dimensions. Enlarging the display size of an image by changing the pixel size in Dreamweaver may cause distortion or blurriness. Reducing the size of an image this way requires visitors to your site to download an image that is larger than necessary. A better way to resize an image is to open it in an image editor such as Adobe Fireworks or Photoshop and change its actual size.

Open an Image in an Image Editor

Adobe designed Dreamweaver to work with multiple image programs so that you can easily open and edit images while you are working on your Web pages. Adobe Fireworks and Photoshop are sophisticated image-editing programs that are designed to make many changes to an image.

Although you can use any image editor, Fireworks and Photoshop are integrated with Dreamweaver because Adobe makes all three programs.

Open an Image in an Image Editor

① Click the image to select it in Dreamweaver.

Note: *You can open any image in an external image editor from within Dreamweaver.*

② Click the Photoshop button (🔲) in the Properties inspector.

You may have to wait a few moments while Photoshop opens.

In Dreamweaver's Preferences, you can associate other image editors, such as Adobe Fireworks.

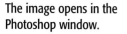

The image opens in the Photoshop window.

You can now edit the image.

③ After making your changes, click **File**.

④ Click **Save As**.

⑤ Save the image with the same name and format, replacing the original image.

Your changes to the image become permanent.

● Photoshop saves the image, and it is automatically updated in the Dreamweaver window.

To edit the image again or to edit another image, you can select the image and repeat steps **2** to **5**.

TIP

What can you do in an image-editing program?

A program such as Adobe Fireworks or Photoshop enables you to edit and combine images to create almost anything that you can imagine. In Dreamweaver's preferences, you can associate Adobe Fireworks, Photoshop, or any other editor on your computer. If you use Fireworks, you can open it to edit an image directly from Dreamweaver by clicking the **Edit/Fireworks Logo** button (or Ps if you use Photoshop).

Add a Background Image

You can insert an image into the background of a Web page to add texture and depth to your design. Background images appear behind any text or images that are on your Web page and are repeated across and down the Web browser window unless you specify otherwise.

Add a Background Image

① Click **Page Properties** in the Properties inspector.

The Page Properties dialog box appears.

② Click **Appearance (CSS)**.

③ Click **Browse**.

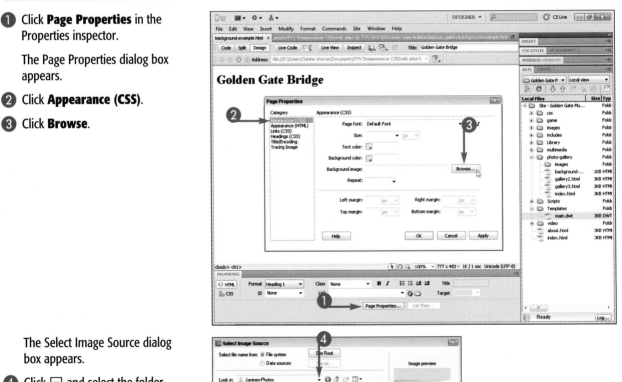

The Select Image Source dialog box appears.

④ Click 🔽 and select the folder that contains the background image file.

⑤ Click the background image that you want to insert.

● A preview image appears.

⑥ Click **OK**.

You are returned to the Page Properties dialog box.

● The image filename and path appear in the **Background Image** text field.

⑦ Click here and choose an option to specify whether or not the image should repeat across and down the page.

⑧ Click **OK**.

The image appears as a background on the Web page.

Note: *The default background setting is for the image to repeat. If the image is smaller than the display area, as in this example, it tiles horizontally and vertically to fill the entire window. You can set the image not to repeat in step 7 to prevent this. You can resize the image in an image editor to adjust its appearance.*

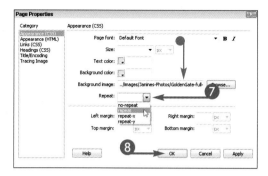

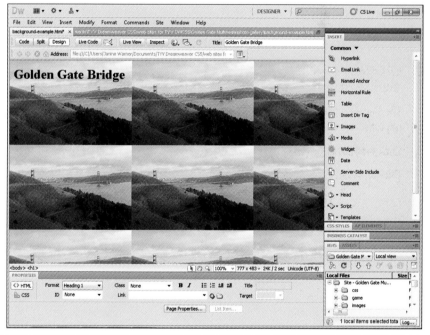

TIPS

What types of images make good backgrounds?

Textures, subtle patterns, and photos with large open areas all make good background images. It is important to make sure that the image does not clash with the text and other content in the foreground or overwhelm the rest of the page. Using an image that tiles seamlessly is also a good idea so that your background appears to be one large image that covers the entire page. Fireworks and Photoshop include a number of features that can help you create background images.

Are backgrounds always patterns?

Although many backgrounds repeat a pattern of some kind, a background image can also be an image that is big enough to fill the entire screen. Because a background image tiles, a vertical image creates a stripe across the top of the page, and a horizontal image creates a left-hand stripe.

Change the Background Color

You can add color to your Web pages by changing the background color. Dreamweaver offers a selection of Web-safe colors that are designed to display well on all computer monitors.

① Click **Page Properties** in the Properties inspector.

The Page Properties dialog box appears.

② Click **Appearance (CSS)**.

③ Click the **Background color** 🔲 to open the color palette (⤢ changes to 🖊).

④ Click a color using the Eyedropper tool (🖊).

⑤ Click **OK**.

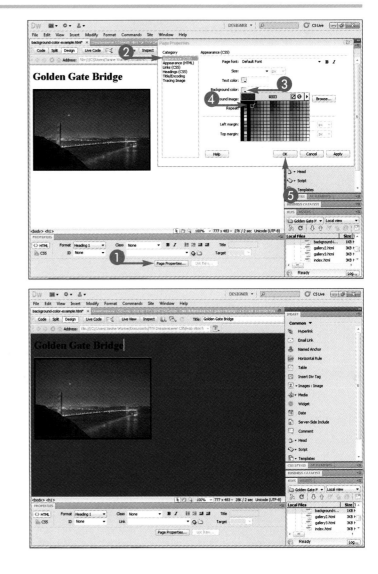

The background of your Web page is displayed in the color that you selected.

Note: For additional information about Web color, see Chapter 12, "Creating and Applying Cascading Style Sheets."

Change Text Colors

You can change the text color for the entire page using Dreamweaver's Page Properties dialog box.

When you alter page and text colors, make sure that the text is still readable. In general, light text colors work best against a dark background, and dark text colors work best against a light background.

The Classic Hawaiian Shirt

Lorem ipsum dolor sit amet, consectetur adipiscing elit, sed do eiusmod tempor incididunt ut labore et dolore magna aliqua. Ut enim ad minim veniam, quis nostrud exercitation ullamco laboris nisi ut aliquip ex ea commodo consequat. Duis aute irure dolor in reprehenderit in voluptate velit esse cillum dolore eu fugiat nulla pariatur. Excepteur sint occaecat cupidatat non proident, sunt in culpa qui officia deserunt mollit anim id est laborum. Lorem ipsum dolor sit amet, consectetur adipiscing elit, sed do eiusmod tempor incididunt ut labore et dolore magna aliqua. Ut enim minim.

Change Text Colors

1 Click **Page Properties** in the Properties inspector.

The Page Properties dialog box appears.

2 Click **Appearance (CSS)**.

3 Click the **Text color** ■ to open the color palette (⟍ changes to ✐).

4 Click a color using the Eyedropper tool (✐).

5 Click **OK**.

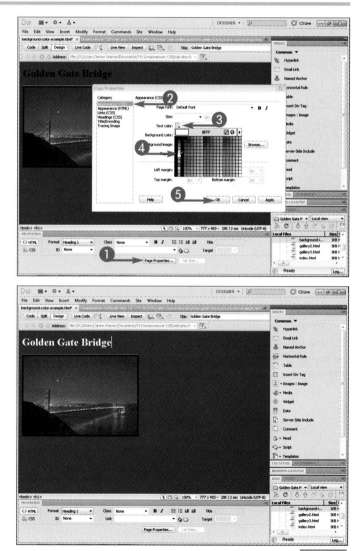

Any text on your Web page is displayed in the color that you selected.

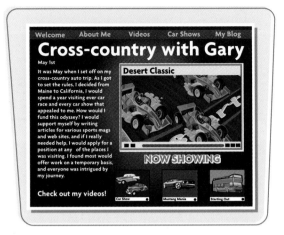

You can add life to your Web page by adding Flash animations and slide shows. A *Flash file* is a multimedia file that is created with Adobe Flash or other software that supports the Flash format with the .swf extension. Flash files are ideal for animated banners, cartoons, slide shows, interactive animations, and site navigation features.

Insert a Flash File

1 Position ◊ where you want to insert a Flash file.

2 Click **Insert**.

3 Click **Media**.

4 Click **SWF**.

● You can also click the **Media** button in the Insert panel and choose **SWF**.

The Select SWF dialog box appears.

5 Click ▾ and select the folder that contains the Flash file.

Note: *Flash filenames end with an .swf file extension.*

6 Click the file that you want to insert into your Web page.

7 Click **OK**.

- A gray box representing the Flash file appears in the Document window.

- You can change the size of the Flash movie by clicking and dragging its lower-left corner or by entering a width and height in the Properties inspector.

⑧ Click **Play** in the Properties inspector to test the Flash file.

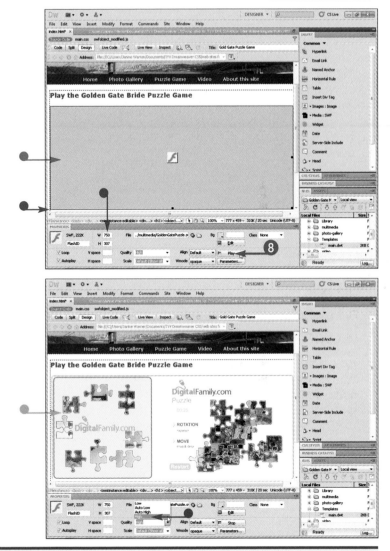

- The Flash file is displayed in your Dreamweaver document.

- You can click the **Quality** ⊡ and select the level of quality at which you want your movie to play.

Note: The higher the quality, the better it is displayed, but then it takes longer to download.

Note: When you save a page after inserting a Flash file, Dreamweaver automatically creates special scripts to help the Flash file play in the Web browser. See the Tip below for more details.

Why do I need scripts to play a Flash File?

When you insert a Flash file into a Web page, Dreamweaver automatically inserts a special script into the code of the page and creates two files that are saved into your main site folder in a folder called *Scripts*. These scripts must be uploaded to your Web server for the Flash file to play properly in a Web browser. Make sure that you upload the entire Scripts folder, as well as the Web page and the Flash file itself, when you publish the site on a Web server. You learn how to publish your site with Dreamweaver's FTP features in Chapter 14, "Publishing a Web Site."

Insert Flash Video Files

You can add audio and video files to Web pages in a variety of formats, including Windows Media Audio and Video and QuickTime. When you insert video and audio files in the Flash format, Dreamweaver provides more options for how the files play in your Web pages. Flash Video files have the .flv extension.

Note: **You must have the Flash Player on your computer to play a Flash Video file. If the Flash Player is not installed, the browser displays a dialog box with instructions for downloading the player.**

Insert Flash Video Files

1 Position ⌖ where you want to insert the Flash Video file in the Document window.

2 Click **Insert**.

3 Click **Media**.

4 Click **FLV**.

● You can also click the **Media** button in the Insert panel and choose **FLV**.

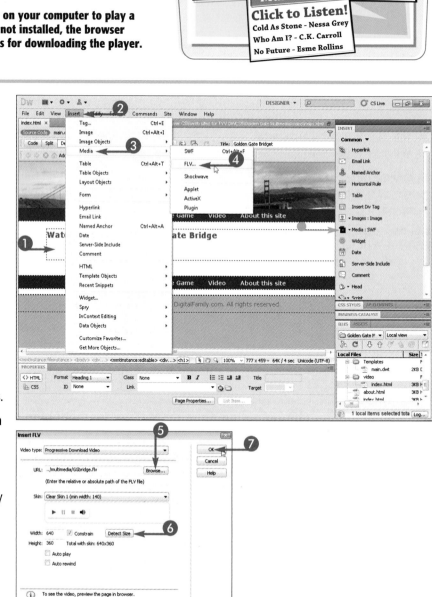

The Insert FLV dialog box appears.

5 Click **Browse** and select the Flash Video file.

Note: *Flash Video filenames end with the .flv file extension.*

6 Click **Detect Size** to automatically enter the height and width.

7 Click **OK**.

The other settings are optional and can be left at the defaults.

● A gray Flash Video box appears in the Document window.

⑧ You can change the Flash Video settings in the Properties inspector.

⑨ Click [▣] to view the page in a Web browser and play the video.

⑩ Click a browser.

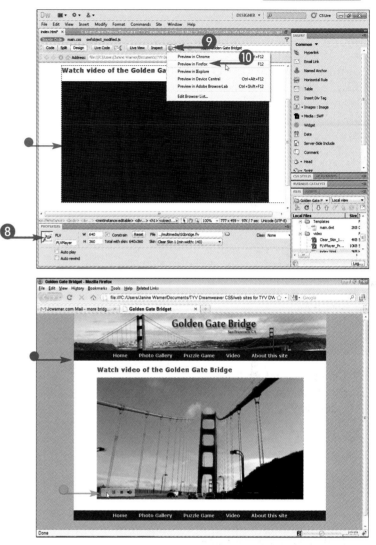

● The selected Web browser opens and displays the Web page.

● When a cursor is rolled over the video, the Flash player controls are displayed.

Note: *When you insert Flash Video, Dreamweaver automatically creates two Flash SWF files for the player controls. For the video to play properly, these files must be uploaded to the server when you upload the video file to your Web server.*

What should I consider when adding multimedia content to my Web site?

Remember that although you may have the latest computer software and a fast connection, some of your visitors may not have the necessary multimedia players or bandwidth for your multimedia files. You can add Flash, video, sound, and other multimedia files to jazz up a Web site, but if your visitors do not have the right programs, they cannot view them. Therefore, it is very important to use compression and other techniques to keep file sizes small and to offer links to players for any multimedia that you use.

Create a Rollover Image

Rollover images are designed to react when someone rolls a cursor over them. They are commonly used in navigation bars and other links, but they can also be used to add a little surprise to your pages. A rollover effect can be subtle or dramatic, depending on the differences between the two images that you use in the rollover, but both images must be the same size.

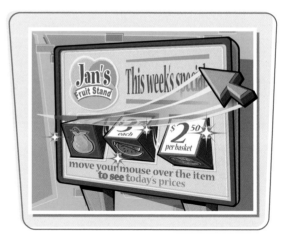

Create a Rollover Image

1. Position 🔓 where you want to insert the rollover image.

2. Click **Insert**.

3. Click **Image Objects**.

4. Click **Rollover Image**.

The Insert Rollover Image dialog box appears.

5. Type an identifying name for scripting purposes.

6. Click **Browse** and select the first image.

7. Click **Browse** and select the second image.

8. Type a description of the images.

9. Type a URL if you want the rollover to serve as a link.

10. Click **OK**.

Dreamweaver automatically inserts the scripting that you need to make the rollover effect work.

● The first image in the rollover is displayed on the page.

⑪ Click 🔲 to view the page in a Web browser and test the rollover effect.

⑫ Click a browser.

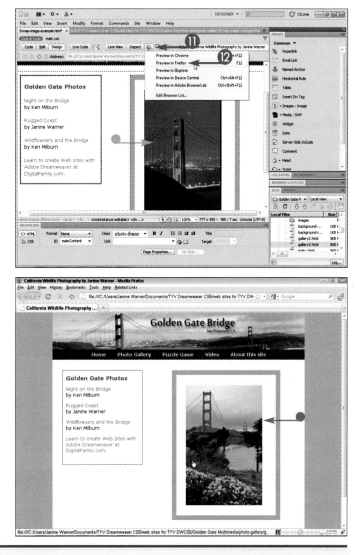

● When you roll your cursor over the first rollover image in a Web browser, the second image appears.

How does the rollover image work?

The interactive effect of a rollover image requires more than HTML. Dreamweaver creates this effect by using a scripting language called *JavaScript*. JavaScript is used for many kinds of interactivity, from image swaps to pop-up windows. JavaScript is more complex than HTML code. Dreamweaver includes many other JavaScript features in the Behaviors panel. To see what other kinds of behaviors are available, click **Window** and then click **Behaviors**.

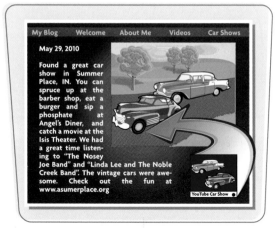

One of the easiest ways to add video to your
Web pages is to embed the video from the
popular video site YouTube, www.youtube.com.
You can embed almost any video on YouTube
into your Web site by copying and pasting a little
code from YouTube into your site.

① In a Web browser, go to
the YouTube Web site,
www.youtube.com.

② Type keywords into the Search
field to find a video that you
want to use.

③ Click **Search**.

Videos that match your search
criteria appear.

④ Select the one that you want to
insert into your Web page.

⑤ Click the Customize button.

The customize options appear.

⑥ Select or deselect the player
options that you want.

⑦ Click a color set for the player.

⑧ Click a size.

⑨ Copy the code from the **Embed**
field.

10 In Dreamweaver, open the Web page into which you want to insert the video.

11 Click **Split** to open the Code and Design views.

12 Click to place your curser in the code where you want the video to appear in the page.

13 Paste the code that you copied from YouTube into Code view in Dreamweaver.

● A gray box appears in the Design area.

14 Click and select a browser to view the page in a Web browser.

● The video is displayed in your Web page in the browser window.

15 Click the Play button to play the video.

Note: You must be connected to the Internet for the video to load from the YouTube site into your Web page.

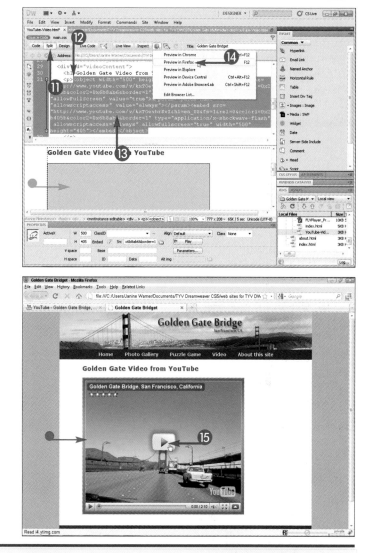

Can I use any videos from YouTube on my site?

YouTube is designed to distribute videos with the broadest possible audience, and most people who use YouTube want to share their videos. Anyone can upload videos to YouTube, and most YouTube users make it possible for you to embed their videos in your Web pages. If someone does not want a video used on your site, he or she can set the privacy options to prevent you from copying the embed code to paste into your Web pages.

Creating Hyperlinks

Links, also called *hyperlinks,* are used to add references to Web pages that take users to another page and trigger some other action, such as launching an email program to send a message. Using Dreamweaver, you can create links from one page to another page in your Web site or to other Web sites on the Internet, and you can also create email links and image maps. This chapter shows you how to create these kinds of links using both text and images.

Link to Other Pages in Your Web Site

Dreamweaver makes it easy to create a link from one page in your Web site to another page so that your visitors can navigate the site easily.

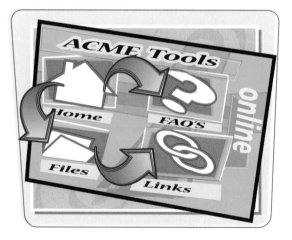

Link to Other Pages in Your Web Site

Create a Link

1. Click and drag to select the text that you want to turn into a link.

2. Click ▼ and choose **Common**.

3. Click the **Hyperlink** 🖉.

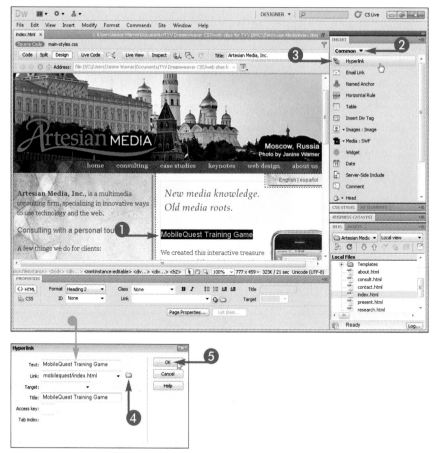

The Hyperlink dialog box appears.

● The selected text is automatically entered in the **Text** field.

4. Click 📁 and select the HTML file to which you want to link.

The other settings in the Hyperlink dialog box are optional.

5. Click **OK**.

● The new link appears in color and underlined.

Note: To change the appearance of links, see the section "Change the Color of Links on a Page" at the end of this chapter.

● The filename and path appear in the **Link** field.

Note: Links are not clickable in the Document window.

● You can click to test the link by previewing the file in a Web browser.

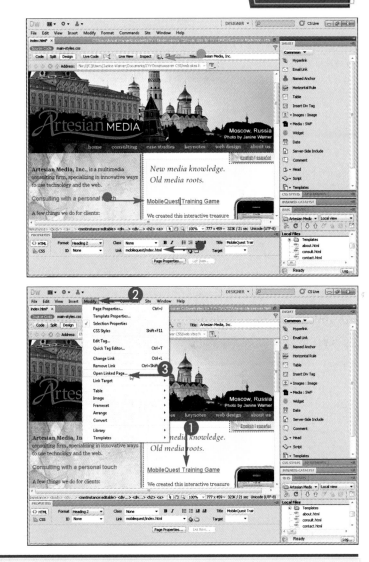

Open and Edit a Linked Page

1 Click anywhere in the text of the link whose destination you want to open.

2 Click **Modify**.

3 Click **Open Linked Page**.

The link destination opens in a Document window, allowing you to edit that document.

TIP

How should I organize the files that make up my Web site?

You should keep all the pages, images, and other files that make up your Web site in one main folder that you define as your local site root folder. This enables you to easily find pages and images and create links between your pages. It also ensures that all the links work correctly when you transfer the files to a Web server. If you have many pages in one section, you can create subfolders in the Files panel to further divide your site's file structure. You may also want to create a separate folder for images. For more information on setting up your Web site, see Chapter 2, "Setting Up Your Web Site." For more information on transferring files to a Web server, see Chapter 14, "Publishing a Web Site."

Link to Another Web Site

You can link from your Web site to any other Web site on the Internet, giving your visitors access to additional information and providing valuable references to related information.

Create a Link

1 Click and drag to select the text that you want to turn into a link.

2 Click ⏷ and choose **Common**.

3 Click the **Hyperlink** 🔖.

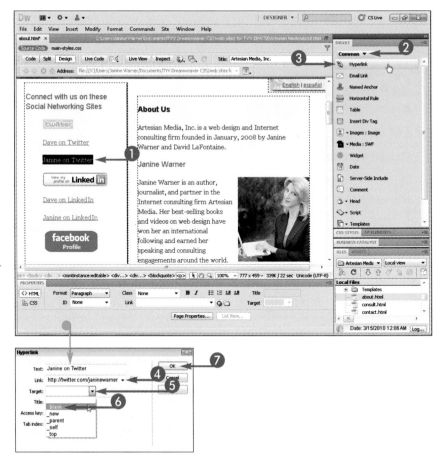

The Hyperlink dialog box appears.

● The selected text is automatically entered in the **Text** field.

4 Type the Web address of the destination page in the **Link** field.

Note: *You must type* **http://** *before the Web address.*

5 Click ⏷.

6 Click **_blank** to create a link that will open in a new browser window or tab.

7 Click **OK**.

● The new link appears in a color and underlined.

Note: *To change the appearance of links, see the section "Change the Color of Links on a Page."*

● The URL appears here.

Note: *Links are not clickable in the Document window.*

● You can click to test the link by previewing the file in a Web browser.

Note: *For more information about previewing a Web page in a browser, see Chapter 2.*

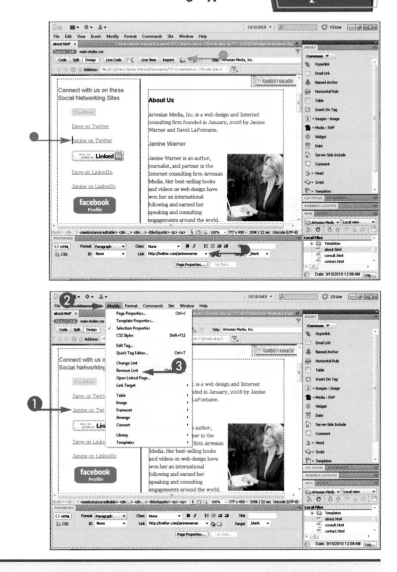

Remove a Link

① Click to place ▷ anywhere in the text of the link that you want to remove.

② Click **Modify**.

③ Click **Remove Link**.

Dreamweaver removes the link, and the text no longer appears in a color and underlined.

TIP

How do I ensure that my links to other Web sites always work?

If you have linked to a Web page whose file is later renamed or taken offline, your viewers receive an error message when they click the link on your Web site. Although you cannot always control the sites to which you link, you can maintain your Web site by periodically viewing your own site in a Web browser and checking to make sure that your links to other sites still work properly. You can also use online services, such as the W3C Link Checker, at http://validator.w3.org/checklink, to perform this check for you. Although neither method can bring back a Web page that no longer exists, you can identify which links you need to remove or update.

Using an Image As a Link

You can use an image to create a link to another page or Web site in much the same way that you create a link with text. Using images as links makes it possible to give visitors to your site more ways to move from page to page.

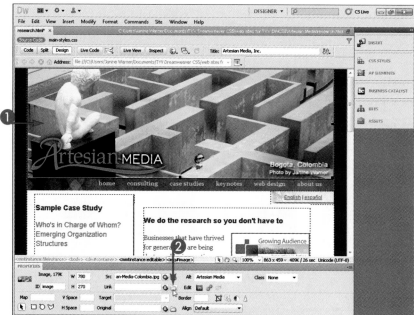

Using an Image As a Link

Create an Image Link

1. Click the image that you want to turn into a link.

2. Click the **Link** 📁.

   You can also use the Hyperlink dialog box, which is available by clicking 📃 in the Common Insert panel and is used in the first two sections of this chapter.

The Select File dialog box appears.

3. Click 🔽 and select the folder that contains the destination page.

4. Click the HTML file to which you want to link.

5. Click **OK**.

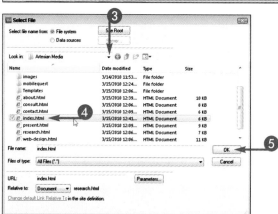

Your image becomes a link.

● Dreamweaver automatically inserts the filename and path to the linked page.

● You can click 🖳 to test the link by previewing your page in a Web browser.

Note: *For more information about previewing a page in a Web browser, see Chapter 2.*

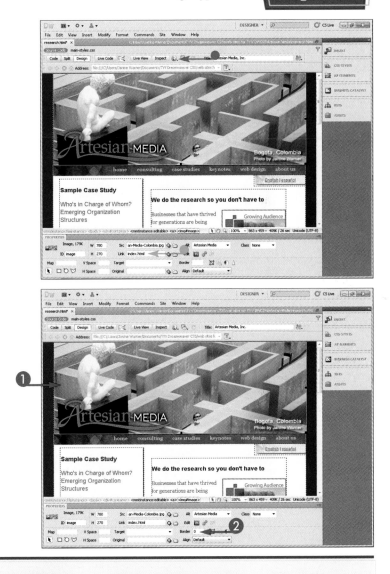

Remove a Border from a LInked Image

1 Click to select the linked image.

2 Type the number **0** in the **Border** field.

3 Press Enter (Return).

The border around the image disappears.

TIPS

How do I create a navigation bar for my Web page?

Many Web sites include a list of links to the main pages or sections of a Web site. This collection of links is commonly called a *navigation bar.* The best place to create these links is at the top, side, or bottom of each page. Including links to the main pages of your site on every page in your site makes it easier for viewers to navigate.

How will visitors to my Web site know to click an image?

When a visitor rolls the cursor over an image that serves as a link, the cursor turns into a hand. You can make it clearer which images are linked by putting links in context with other content and by grouping links to let visitors know that images are clickable.

Create a Jump Link within a Page

You can create a link to other content on the same page. Same-page links, often called *jump links* or *anchor links,* are commonly used on long pages when you want to provide an easy way to navigate to relevant information lower on the page.

You create a jump link by first placing a named anchor where you want the link to go to and then linking from the text or image to the named anchor point.

Create a Jump Link within a Page

1. Position ⌖ where you want to insert the named anchor.

2. Click ▼ and choose **Common**.

3. Click the **Named Anchor** 🔖.

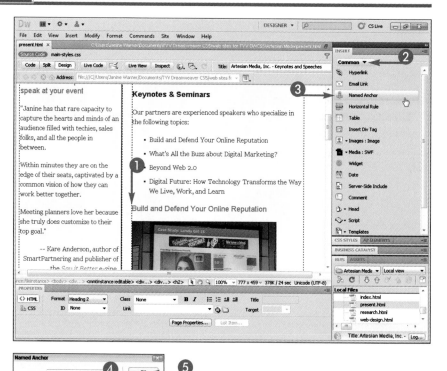

The Named Anchor dialog box appears.

4. Type a name for the anchor.

5. Click **OK**.

- An anchor appears in the Document window.

⑥ Click and drag to select the text that you want to link to the anchor.

⑦ Click in the Common Insert panel.

The Hyperlink dialog box appears.

⑧ Click the **Link** ▾.

⑨ Click the anchor name.

⑩ Click **OK**.

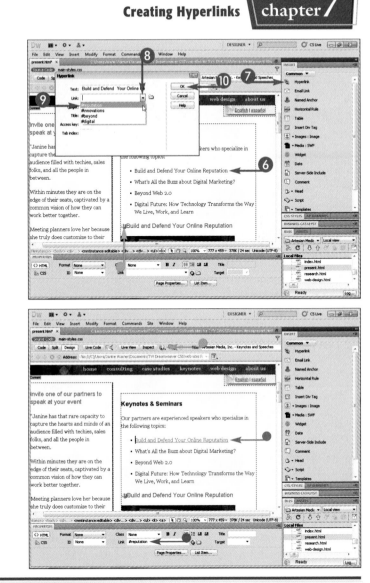

- The text appears as a link on the page.

- The anchor name appears in the **Link** field, preceded by a pound (#) sign.

Note: Links are not clickable in the Document window.

- You can click 🖉 to test the link by previewing the file in a Web browser.

Note: For more information about previewing a page in a Web browser, see Chapter 2.

TIP

Why would I create a jump link to something on the same page?

Web designers use jump links to make it easier to find text that appears lower on a page. These links are frequently used on very long pages to give visitors an easy way to return to the top of a page by clicking a jump link lower on the page. Similarly, if you have a Web page that has many sections of information, jump links enable you to link to each section from a link menu at the top of the page. A frequently asked questions (FAQ) page is another example of when to use same-page links; you can list all your questions at the top of the page and link to the answers lower on the page.

Create a Link to Another File Type

Links do not have to lead just to other Web pages. You can also link to other file types, such as image files, word-processing documents, PDF files, and multimedia files. Many of these files require their own players, but as long as your visitor has the required program, the file opens automatically when the user clicks the link.

Create a Link to Another File Type

1 Click and drag to select the text that you want to turn into a link.

2 Click ▼ and choose **Common**.

3 Click the **Hyperlink** 🔖.

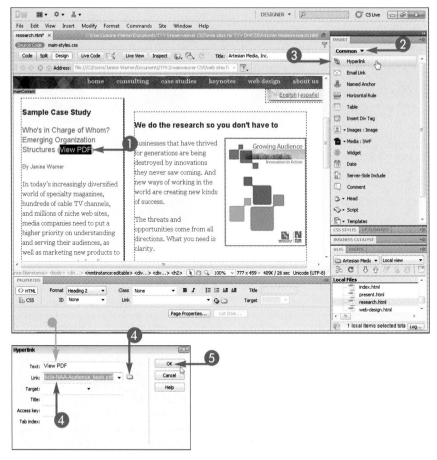

The Hyperlink dialog box appears.

● The selected text is automatically entered in the **Text** field.

4 To link to a file on another Web site, type the Web address of the destination page.

OR

4 To link to a file on your own site, click 📁 and select the file to which you want to link.

The rest of the settings are optional.

5 Click **OK**.

● The text appears as a link on the page.

Note: Links are not clickable in the Document window.

⑥ Click 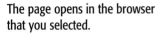 and select a Web browser.

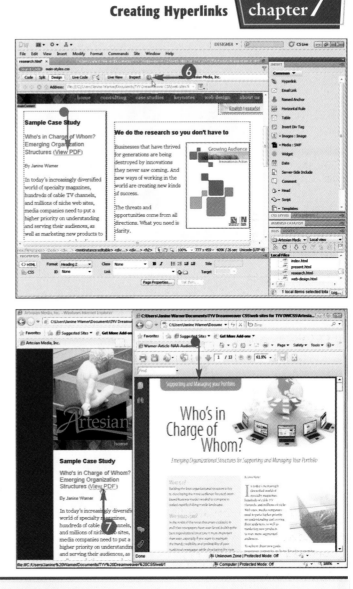

The page opens in the browser that you selected.

⑦ Click the link.

● The linked file opens.

In this example, a PDF document opens in the Web browser window.

Create an Image Map

You can link different areas of an image to different pages with an image map. First, you define areas of the image, called *hotspots*, using Dreamweaver's image-mapping tools, and then you turn them into links.

Create an Image Map

① Click the image.

② Type a name for the image map.

***Note:** You cannot use spaces or special characters.*

③ Click a drawing tool.

You can create rectangular shapes with the Rectangular Hotspot tool (□), oval shapes with the Oval Hotspot tool (○), and irregular shapes with the Polygon Hotspot tool (▽).

④ Draw an area on the image that will serve as a hotspot for a link.

● If a message appears instructing you to describe the image map in the Alt field, click **OK** to close the dialog box, type a description in the **Alt** field, and then resume drawing the hotspot area over the image.

● To link to another Web site, type the URL into the **Link** field.

⑤ Click ▭.

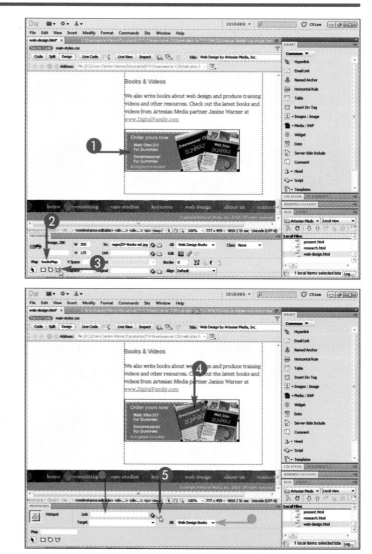

The Select File dialog box appears.

⑥ Click ▼ and select the folder that contains the destination file.

⑦ Click the file to which you want to link.

⑧ Click **OK**.

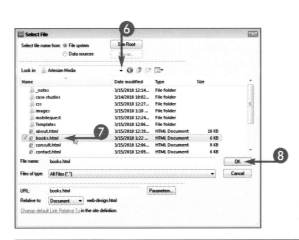

● The hotspot area defined by the selected shape is linked to the selected file, and the name and path to the file are displayed when the hotspot is selected.

To delete a hotspot, you can select it and then press Del.

You can repeat steps **3** to **8** to add other linked areas to your image.

Note: The image-map shapes do not appear when you open the page in a browser, but clicking anywhere in a hotspot area will trigger the corresponding link.

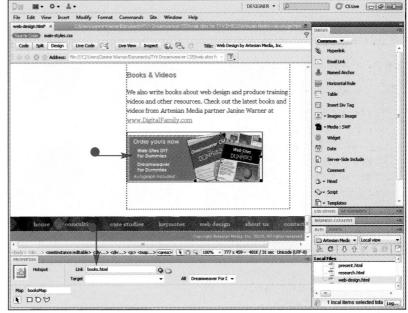

Can image maps be used for geographical maps that link to multiple locations?

Yes. An interactive geographical map, such as a map of Latin America, is a common place to see hotspots in action. You can create one by adding a graphic image of a map to your Web page and then defining a hotspot over each location to which you want to link. Use the Polygon tool (▽) to draw around boundaries that do not follow a square or circular shape. Then link each hotspot to a page with information about the corresponding geographic region.

Create a Link Using the Files Panel

Dreamweaver provides multiple options for creating links. For example, you can create links quickly and easily using the Point to File button in the Properties inspector to select a file in the Files panel.

Your Web pages are displayed in the Files panel only if you have set up your Web site in Dreamweaver, an important first step that is covered in Chapter 2.

Create a Link Using the Files Panel

*Note: Make sure that both the Document window and the Files panel are visible and that **HTML** is selected in the Properties inspector.*

① Click and drag to select the text that you want to turn into a link.

② Click the Point to File button (⬚).

③ Drag the cursor until it is over the file that you want to link to in the Files panel.

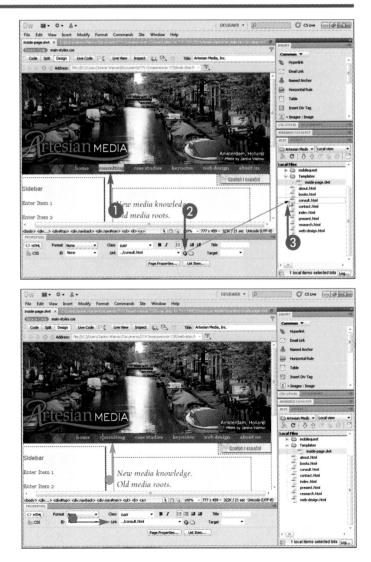

● The text appears as a link on the page.

Note: You can change the appearance of links by following the steps in the section "Change the Color of Links on a Page."

● The name and path to the file you linked to are displayed in the **Link** field in the Properties inspector.

You can create a link that, when clicked, opens a new Web browser window to display the destination page.

Opening a new browser window allows a user to keep the previous Web page open.

Open a Linked Page in a New Browser Window

1. Click and drag to select the link that you want to open in a new browser window.

2. Click the **Target** ⏷.

3. Click **_blank**.

4. Click 🔲 and select a Web browser to preview the page.

The page opens in the browser that you selected.

5. Click the link.

● The link destination appears in a new browser window, and the page with the link remains open behind the linked page.

Note: *If the user's browser window is set to fill the entire screen, the original Web page will not be visible when the linked page is opened.*

You can create an email link on your Web page. When a user clicks the link, it launches the email program on the user's computer, creates a message, and inserts the email address into the Address field.

① Click to select the text or image that you want to turn into an email link.

② Click the **Email Link** button (☐).

Note: If ☐ is not visible, choose **Common** from the drop-down list.

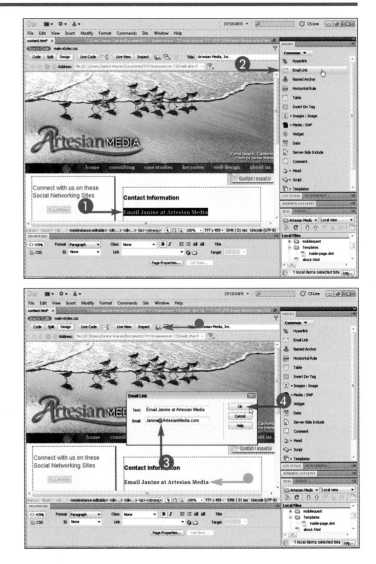

The Email Link dialog box appears, with the selected text in the Text field.

③ Type the email address to which you want to link.

④ Click **OK**.

● Dreamweaver creates your email link, and the selected text is displayed as a link.

● To test the link, you can click 📷 and select a Web browser to preview the page.

Note: For an email link to work properly, the user must have an email program installed on his or her computer.

Check Links

You can automatically verify the links in a Web site. Using Dreamweaver's link-testing features, you can generate a report that lists any links that are broken within the site, as well as links to other sites that should be tested in a browser.

There are many ways that links can become broken. Dreamweaver makes it easy to find and fix them.

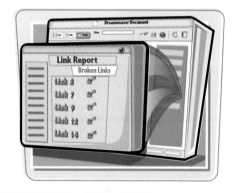

Check Links

① Click **Site**.

② Click **Check Links Sitewide**.

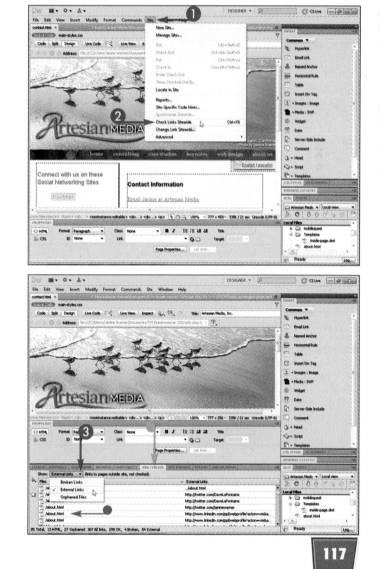

● Dreamweaver checks all the links and lists all broken links, external links, and orphaned files.

③ Click ▼ and select the type of links you want displayed.

Note: *Dreamweaver cannot verify links to Web pages on external sites.*

● To correct a broken link, double-click the file to open it, select the linked item, and click the **Browse** 🗀 to reset the link correctly.

Change the Color of Links on a Page

You can change the color of the links on your Web page to make them match the visual style of the other text and images on your page. You can also remove the underline under linked text.

Change the Color of Links on a Page

1. Click **Modify**.

2. Click **Page Properties**.

● You can also click **Page Properties** in the Properties inspector.

The Page Properties dialog box appears.

3. Click the **Active links** 📧 (⬚ changes to 🖊).

4. Click a color from the menu using the 🖊 tool.

5. Repeat steps **3** and **4** to specify colors for **Link color**, **Visited links**, and **Rollover links**.

● You can click the Color Picker (📧) to select a custom color.

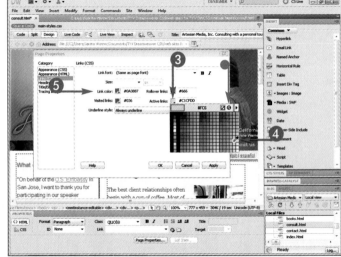

6 Click the **Underline Style** ▼.

7 Click **Never Underline** to remove the underline from all of your links.

8 Click **OK**.

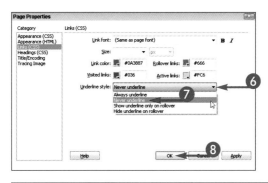

● The links are displayed in the specified link color and underline option.

What color will my links be if I do not choose colors for them?

Blue is the default link color in the Dreamweaver Document window. What viewers see when the page opens in a Web browser depends on their browser settings. By default, most Web browsers display unvisited links as blue, visited links as purple, and rollover links as red.

What do each of the link options in the Page Properties dialog box represent?

Link color represents the display color for a link that has not yet been clicked by a site visitor; **Visited links** represents the color a link changes to after it has been clicked; **Rollover links** represents the display color a link changes to as a visitor rolls a cursor over it; and **Active links** represents the display color a link changes to when a visitor is actively clicking it.

CHAPTER 8

Editing the Table Design in a Web Page

Tables are an ideal way to format tabular data, such as the information that you find in a spreadsheet. You can also use tables to create designs with multiple columns, even within the constraints of HTML. This chapter shows you how to create and format tables.

Insert a Table into a Web Page

You can use tables to organize and design pages that contain financial data, text, images, and multimedia. Dreamweaver's layout features enable you to create tables for tabular data, simple layouts, and other design features. You can even insert tables inside other tables.

Insert a Table

1. Position ⬚ where you want to insert a table.

   By default, the cursor snaps to the left margin, although you can change the table alignment.

2. Click the **Table** 📧 in the Common Insert panel.

● You can also click **Insert** and then click **Table**.

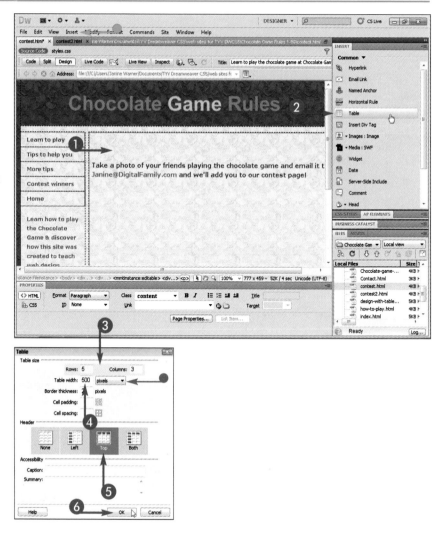

   The Table dialog box appears.

3. Type the number of rows and columns that you want in your table.

4. Type the width of your table.

● You can set the width in pixels or as a percentage of the page by clicking 🔽 and selecting your choice of measurements.

5. Click to select a table Header option.

6. Click **OK**.

● An empty table appears, aligned to the left by default.

⑦ Click ▾.

⑧ Click an alignment option.

The table aligns on the page.

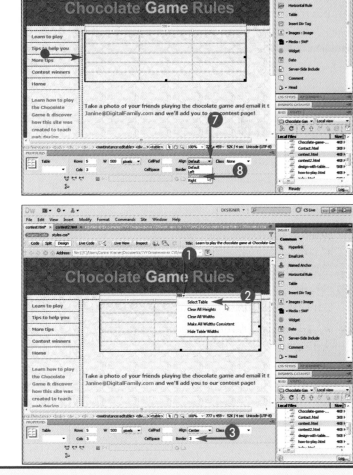

Edit the Table Border

① Click ▾.

② Click **Select Table**.

③ Type the number of pixels of border thickness you want in the **Border** field.

④ Press Enter (Return).

If you set the border to 0, Dreamweaver will replace the visible border with a dashed line to show you the borders in the workspace. When you view the page in a Web browser, the dashed table border disappears.

TIPS

Why are table headers important for accessibility?

The Table Header setting designates a row or column of a table as the content that describes the information in the rest of the table. It also provides additional information about the importance of the header content. This setting is used by *screen readers,* which are special Web browsers that are used by the blind or visually impaired, to help describe the table when the text in the table is read aloud.

Why would I turn off table borders?

Table borders can help to define the edges of a table and to organize columnar data, such as a financial report. However, if you want to use a table to arrange photos and text within the design of your page, you can have a cleaner layout if you set the border to zero so that it becomes invisible. You can set the table border to one pixel for a slim border or try five or ten pixels if you want a thick border.

Insert Content into a Table

You can fill the cells of your table with text, images, multimedia files, form elements, and even other tables, just as you would add them anywhere else on a Web page.

Insert Content into a Table

Insert Text

① Click to place your cursor inside the table cell.

② Type text into the cell.

Note: To format your text, see Chapter 5, "Formatting and Styling Text."

Insert an Image

① Click inside the table cell.

② Click the **Image** button ().

The Select Image Source dialog box appears.

③ Click ▼ and select the folder that contains your image.

④ Click the image file.

⑤ Click **OK**.

If the Image Tag Accessibility Attributes dialog box opens, enter a description of the image in the **Alt** field. The Accessibility Attributes dialog box can be turned on and off in the program's Preferences.

● The image appears in the table cell.

● If the image is larger than the cell, the cell expands to accommodate the image.

● You can click to select the image to display the image settings in the Properties inspector.

Note: To edit your image, see Chapter 6, "Working with Images and Multimedia."

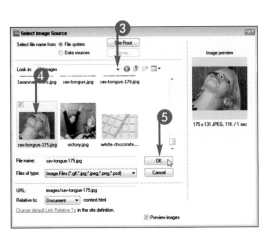

How do I change the appearance of the content inside my table?

You can specify the size, style, and color of text inside a table in the same way that you format text on a Web page. Similarly, you can control the appearance of an image inside a table in the same way that you can control it outside a table. For more information on formatting text, see Chapter 5; for more information on images, see Chapter 6.

Change the Background Color of a Table

You can change the background color of a table or only change the background color of a cell, a row, or a column. This is a great way to add a design element or to call attention to a section of a table. For more information on Web page backgrounds, see Chapter 6.

Change the Background Color of a Table

Using the Color Palette

1 Click 🔽 and click **Select Table** to select the entire table, or click an individual cell, or click and drag to select a row or column of cells.

2 Click the **Bg** 🔳.

3 Click a color.

● You can click the Color Picker button (🔘) to select a custom color.

● Click the Default Color button (🔲) to remove a specified color.

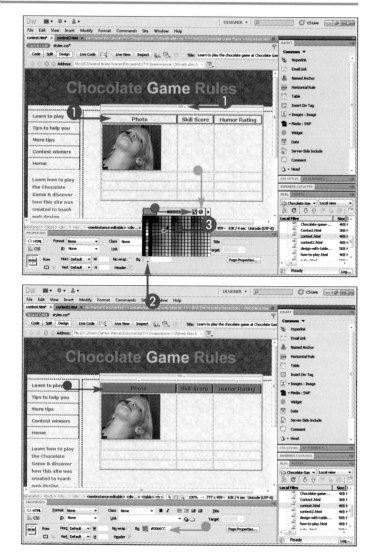

● The color fills the background of the selected cells.

● You can also type a color name or hexadecimal color code into the color field.

Note: To change the font color on a Web page, see Chapter 12, "Creating and Applying Cascading Style Sheets."

Using a Color from Your Web Page

1. Click and click **Select Table** to select the entire table, or click an individual cell, or click and drag to select a row or column of cells.

2. Click the **Bg** ■ to open the color palette (⟍ changes to ✐).

3. Click a color anywhere on the screen to select it.

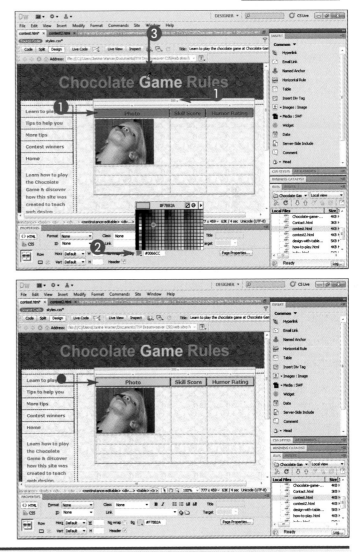

● The selected table cells' background fills with the color that you clicked.

How can I change the background of an entire table?

To change the color of an entire table, you can click to select all the cells in a table and then choose a background color that will apply to all the cells. A better way is to create a style rule for the Table tag using cascading style sheets (CSS) and specify a background image or color as part of that style. You find out how to create styles in Chapter 12.

Change the Cell Padding in a Table

You can change the cell padding to add space between a table's content and its borders.

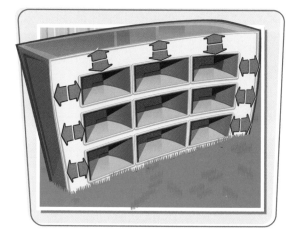

① Click ▣ and click **Select Table** to select the entire table.

② In the **CellPad** field in the Properties inspector, type the amount of padding that you want in pixels.

③ Press Enter (Return).

The space changes between the table content and the table borders.

Note: *Adjusting the cell padding affects all the cells in a table. You cannot adjust the padding of individual cells by using the CellPad field.*

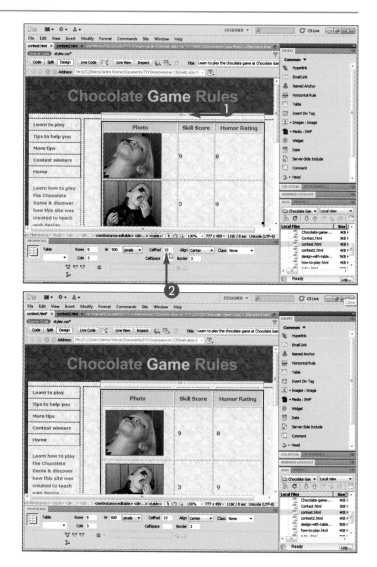

Change the Cell Spacing in a Table

You can change cell spacing to adjust the distance that cells are from each other.

Change the Cell Spacing in a Table

① Click  and click **Select Table** to select the entire table.

② In the **CellSpace** field, type the amount of spacing that you want in pixels.

③ Press Enter (Return).

The cell spacing changes.

● You can change the width of the table or a column by clicking and dragging the cell borders.

Note: *Adjusting the cell spacing affects all the cell borders in the table. You cannot adjust the spacing of individual cell borders by using the CellSpace field.*

Insert a Table inside a Table Cell

You can insert a table into the cell of another table in much the same way as you insert a table into a Web page.

Insert a Table inside a Table Cell

① Click inside the table cell.

② Click the **Table** button (▦).

The Table dialog box appears.

③ Type values in the fields to define the characteristics of the table.

④ Click **OK**.

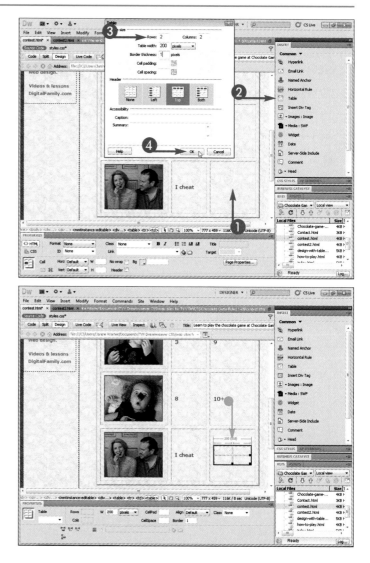

● The new table appears within the table cell.

You can align the content in your table cells horizontally and vertically. For example, you can center elements or move them to the top or bottom of a cell.

Change the Alignment of Cell Content

1 Click and drag to select an entire column or row.

You can press **Shift** + click, or click and drag, to select multiple cells.

2 Click the **Horz** ▼ to change the alignment horizontally.

3 Click an alignment.

To change the vertical alignment, repeat steps **1** to **3**, clicking the **Vert** ▼ in step **2**.

● The content aligns within the cells.

In this example, horizontal alignment is used to align the text in these cells in the center.

Insert or Delete a Row or Column

You can insert cells into your table to add content or to create space between elements. You can also delete rows or columns to remove them when they are not needed.

Insert a Row or Column

1 Click ⊡ and click **Select Table** to select the entire table.

2 Type the number of rows or columns that you want to insert in the Properties inspector.

3 Press Enter (Return).

● Empty rows or columns appear in the table.

To add a row or column in the middle of a table, you can right-click inside an existing cell, click **Table**, and then click **Insert Row** or **Insert Column** from the menu that appears.

● You can also click **Modify**, click **Table**, and then click **Insert Row** or **Insert Column**.

Delete a Row or Column

1 Select the cells that you want to delete by pressing Shift + clicking or clicking and dragging over them.

2 Press Del.

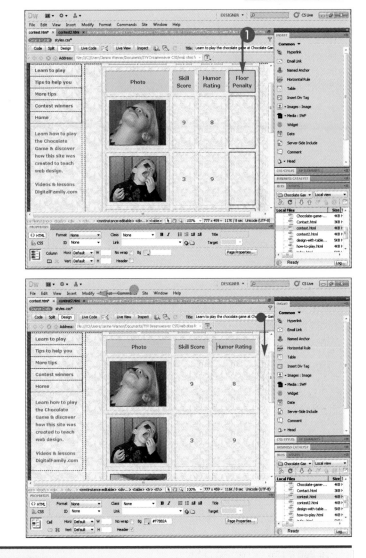

● The selected table cells disappear.

Note: *The content of a cell is deleted when you delete the cell.*

You can also delete cells by right-clicking inside the cells, clicking **Table**, and then clicking either **Delete Row** or **Delete Column** from the menu.

● You can also click **Modify**, click **Table**, and then click either **Delete Row** or **Delete Column**.

TIPS

Does Dreamweaver warn me if a deleted cell contains content?

No, Dreamweaver does not warn you if the cells that you are deleting in a table contain content. This is because Dreamweaver assumes that you also want to delete the cell content. If you accidentally remove content when deleting rows or columns, you can click **Edit** and then click **Undo** to undo your last action.

How do I move content around a table?

You can move the contents of a table cell by clicking to select any image, text, or element in the cell and then dragging it out of the table or into another cell. You can also use the Copy and Paste commands to move content from one cell to another or to another part of a page.

Split or Merge Table Cells

You can create more elaborate page designs by splitting or merging cells in a table to create larger cells adjacent to smaller ones. You can then insert text, images, and other content into the cells.

Split a Table Cell

① Click to place your cursor in the cell that you want to split.

② Click the Split Cell button () in the Properties inspector.

● You can also split a cell by clicking **Modify**, clicking **Table**, and then clicking **Split Cell**.

Alternatively, you can split a cell by right-clicking (**Control** + clicking) inside it, clicking **Table**, and then clicking **Split Cell**.

The Split Cell dialog box appears.

③ Click **Rows** or **Columns**, depending on which you want to use to split the cell (◉ changes to ◉).

④ Type the number of rows or columns.

⑤ Click **OK**.

● The table cell splits.

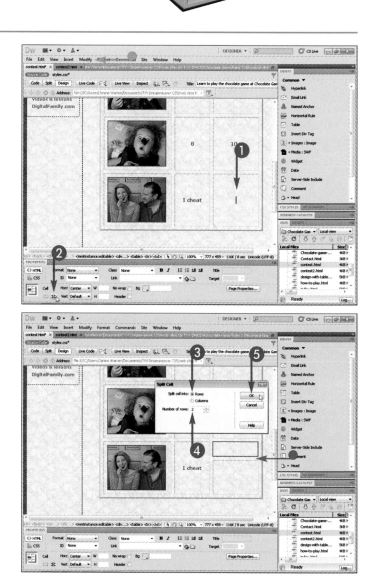

Merge Table Cells

① Click and drag to select the cells that you want to merge.

② Click the Merge button (▣) in the Properties inspector.

● You can also merge cells by clicking **Modify**, clicking **Table**, and then clicking **Merge Cells**.

Alternatively, you can merge cells by right-clicking (Control + clicking) inside them, clicking **Table**, and then clicking **Merge Cells**.

● The table cells merge.

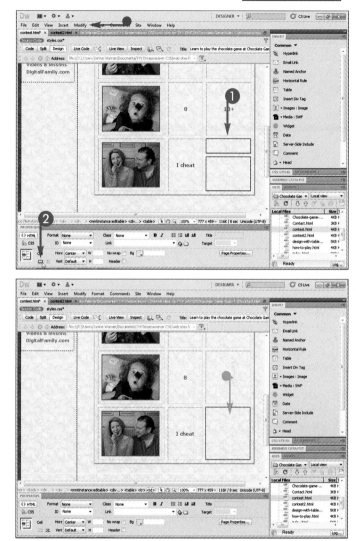

Can I merge any combination of table cells?

No. The cells must have a rectangular arrangement. For example, you can merge all the cells in a two-row-by-two-column table. However, you cannot select three cells that form an *L* shape and merge them into one cell.

Can I add as many cells as I want?

Yes, just make sure that your final table design displays well on a computer monitor. For example, although it is common to design Web pages that are long and require visitors to scroll down, it can be confusing to create overly wide pages that require scrolling right or left. Keep your overall page width under 760 pixels wide if you want it to display well on an 800 x 600 resolution computer monitor or under 1000 for a resolution of 1024 x 760.

You can change the dimensions of individual table cells to better accommodate their content. As you enlarge and reduce cells, you can create more complex tables for more precise design control.

Change the Dimensions of a Cell

1 Click to select the edge of a cell and drag to adjust the size.

2 Press **Enter** (**Return**).

● The cell and its contents readjust to its new dimensions.

● You can also click to place your cursor inside a cell and then enter a size in the **W** (width) or **H** (height) fields in the Properties inspector.

Note: Cell dimensions may be constrained by content. For example, Dreamweaver cannot shrink a cell smaller than the size of the content that it contains.

You can change the dimensions of your entire table. This helps you to ensure that your content fits well within your Web page.

Change the Dimensions of a Table

① Click ▼ and click **Select Table** to select the entire table.

② Type a width.

③ Click ▼ and select the width setting in pixels or a percentage of the screen.

④ Press Enter (Return).

● The table readjusts to its new dimensions.

Note: *Table dimensions may be constrained by content. For example, Dreamweaver cannot shrink a table smaller than the size of an image that it contains.*

If you do not specify a height or width, the table automatically adjusts to fit the space that is available on the user's screen.

Using Percentages for Table Width

You can specify the size of a table using percentage instead of pixels. As a result, the table automatically adjusts to fit a user's browser window size.

When you define a table size as a percentage, it adjusts to fill that percentage of a user's browser window. If the new table is inside another table or other container, it adjusts within the container's boundaries.

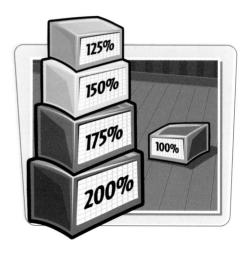

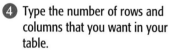

Using Percentages for Table Width

Set Table Width As a Percentage

1. Position Ⓚ where you want to insert the table.

   By default, the cursor snaps to the left margin, although you can change the table alignment.

Note: *For instructions on creating a table, see the section "Insert a Table into a Web Page."*

2. Click **Insert**.

3. Click **Table**.

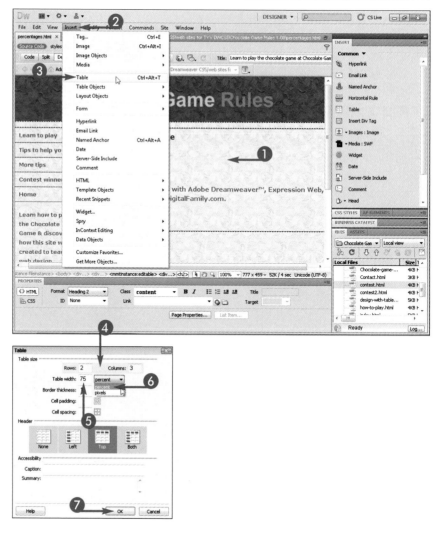

The Table dialog box appears.

4. Type the number of rows and columns that you want in your table.

5. Type the percentage of width that you want your table to fill in the browser window.

6. Click ⏷ and select **percent**.

7. Click **OK**.

● An empty table appears, aligned to the left by default, and fills the available window, based on the percentage width that you specified.

● You can click here and enter a different percentage.

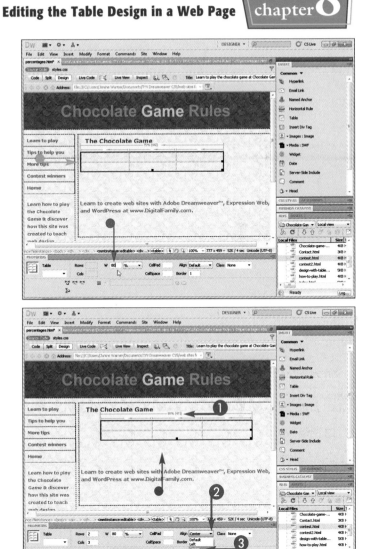

Center a Table

1 Click ▼ and click **Select Table** to select the entire table.

2 Click the **Align** ▼.

3 Click **Center**.

● The table aligns in the center of the page.

TIPS

What is a spacer image?

A spacer image is a transparent GIF image file that is used as a filler to invisibly control spacing on a Web page. You insert a spacer image into a table cell and use the height and width attributes to control its size. This ensures that blank spaces on your page remain consistent. This is important because Web browsers sometimes display elements closer together if there is no text or image to maintain consistent spacing within the design.

How do you make a spacer image?

You can create your own spacer image in an image-editing program, such as Adobe Photoshop or Fireworks. Create a new image and set the background color to transparent. Save it as a GIF file in your Web site folder. An ideal size for a spacer image is 10 pixels by 10 pixels; however, it can be any size. You can resize it in Dreamweaver to fit the space that you want to fill.

Format a Table with CSS

Although you can use table attributes to adjust the formatting and alignment of tables and table cells, as shown earlier in this chapter, you can also create styles to format a table.

Cascading style sheets offer many advantages. Although working with styles is more complex at first, using styles instead of table attributes creates cleaner, more efficient code and makes it easier to change the table formatting later.

1. Click **Format**.
2. Click **CSS Styles**.
3. Click **New**.

The New CSS Rule dialog box appears.

4. Click ▼.
5. Click **Tag**.
6. Type **table**.

● Alternatively, you can click ▼ and choose the tag name **table** from the drop-down list.

7. Click **OK**.

The CSS Rule Definition dialog box appears.

⑧ Click **Border**.

⑨ Specify the border settings that you want.

● You can specify many other formatting settings in this dialog box by selecting other categories, such as **Type**.

⑩ Click **OK**.

● The style is automatically applied to the table in the page.

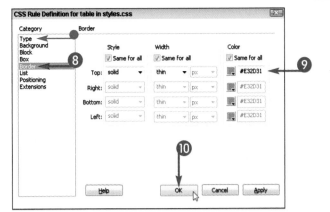

Can I do all of my table formatting with CSS?
You can create rules using cascading style sheets to redefine all of the table tags. The table tags include <table>, the main tag; <th> for table header; <tr> for table row; and <td> for table data cell. By defining rules in CSS for each of these table tags, you can change the size, alignment, background and text colors, and other formatting options for the entire table. The advantage? You can use the same styles for all the tables in your site, making formatting quicker and easier and your code cleaner and faster to download.

Creating Pages with Frames

You can divide the display area of a Web browser into multiple panes by creating frames. Frames offer another way to organize information by splitting up your pages. For example, you can keep linked content visible in one frame and target it to open in a different frame within the same browser window.

Introducing Frames

Frames enable you to divide a Web page into multiple sections and display different pages in each frame.

Although frames are no longer recommended for most sites, they are still used on the Web, and Dreamweaver includes a special feature set for working with them. You can create links in one frame and have the links open their destination pages in another frame.

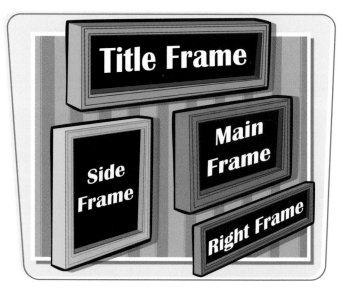

Set Up a Frame

You can create a framed Web site in Dreamweaver by dividing the Document window horizontally or vertically one or more times. Each frame is composed of a different Web page that you can link independently. All pages in a frameset are identified in a *frameset page,* and you must save them separately.

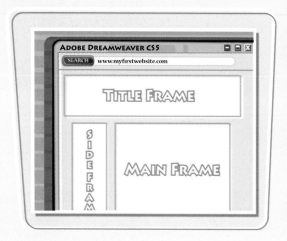

How Frames Work

Frames on a page operate independently of one another. As you scroll through the content of one frame, the content of the other frames remains fixed. You can create a link in one frame and target the link to open in any other frame.

Open the Frames Panel

Dreamweaver includes a number of features designed to make it easy to work with frames. One of the most important is the Frames panel.

As you work with frames, keep the Frames panel open. It is a handy tool for helping you identify and target which frames you are working on as you develop your site.

Open the Frames Panel

① Click **Window**.

② Click **Frames**.

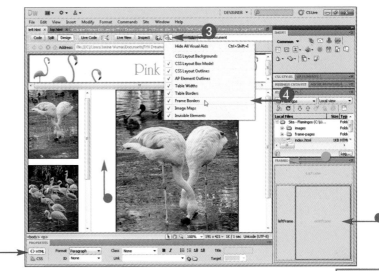

● The Frames panel appears.

● You can click in a corresponding frame in the Frames panel to select it in the workspace.

● The Properties inspector displays the settings for the selected frame.

③ Click the Visual Aids button (🖾).

④ If there is no ☑ next to **Frame Borders**, click to select it.

The frame borders become visible in the Design pane.

Insert a Predefined Frameset

You can easily create popular frame styles using the predefined framesets. You can access frame styles from the Frames tab in the Insert panel. They are also available in the Page from Sample framesets in the New Document dialog box.

Insert a Predefined Frameset

1 Click **File**.

2 Click **New**.

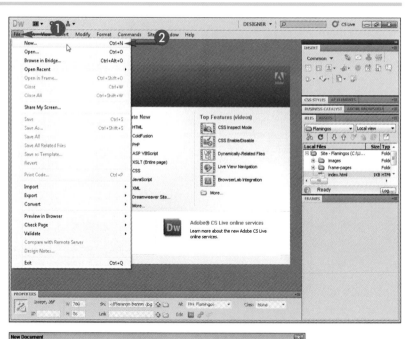

The New Document dialog box appears.

3 Click **Page from Sample**.

4 Click the **Frameset** .

5 Click a frameset design.

● A preview of the selected frameset is displayed here.

6 Click **Create**.

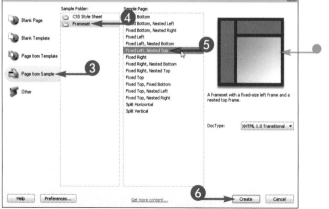

The Frame Tag Accessibility Attributes dialog box appears.

⑦ Click ▼ and select the frame to which you want to add a title.

⑧ Type a title for the frame or accept the frame title automatically assigned.

⑨ Click **OK**.

⑩ Repeat steps **7** to **9** for each frame.

● You can turn disability features off in Dreamweaver's Preferences by clicking this link.

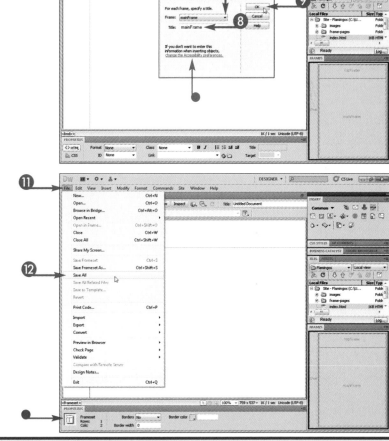

Dreamweaver automatically creates all the frames in the work area and assigns each frame a name.

● The frameset properties appear in the Properties inspector.

⑪ Click **File**.

⑫ Click **Save All**.

Note: You must save each frame in a frameset individually in the Save As dialog box.

TIPS

Can I save individual pages in my frameset separately?

Yes. Saving a frameset requires you to save each of the individual pages that appear in the frames, as well as the frameset that defines how each frame appears. However, you can save any of the pages within a frameset individually. Simply click to place ⌖ in the frame area that you want to save, click **File**, and then click **Save**. Dreamweaver saves only the page that you selected.

What steps do I take if I want to change just one frame?

You can open any existing page in an area of a frameset. Place ⌖ in the frame that you want to change, click **File**, and then click **Open** to open an existing page. You can also click **File** and then click **New** to create a new page in any frame area.

Divide a Page into Frames

You can split a Document window vertically to create a frameset with left and right frames, or you can split it horizontally to create a frameset with top and bottom frames. You can also combine them to create more complex frames or add frames to a predefined frameset.

1 Click **Modify**.

2 Click **Frameset**.

3 Click a **Split Frame** command.

● The window splits into two frames. If content existed in the original page, it shifts to one of the new frames.

Note: Which frame it shifts to depends on the command that you chose in step 3.

● Scroll bars appear if the content extends outside the frame borders.

Create a Nested Frame

You can subdivide a frame of an existing frameset to create nested frames. With nested frames, you can organize the information in your site in a more complex way.

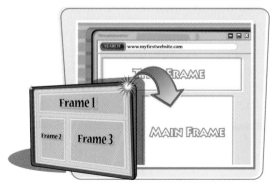

Create a Nested Frame

1. Click inside the frame that you want to subdivide.

2. Click **Modify**.

3. Click **Frameset**.

4. Click a **Split Frame** command.

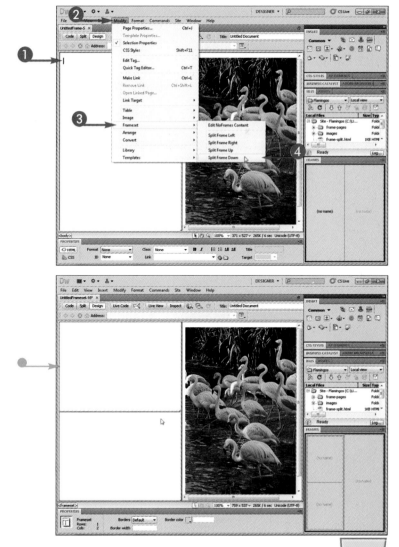

● Dreamweaver splits the selected frame into two frames, creating a nested frame.

Note: How it splits the frame depends on the command that you chose in step **4**.

You can continue to split your frames into more frames.

Change the Attributes of a Frame

You can change the dimensions of a frame to display the information more attractively inside it. You can also change scrolling and other options in the Properties inspector.

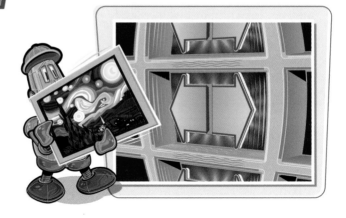

Change the Attributes of a Frame

Specify a Column Size

1 Click the frame that you want to change in the Frames panel.

*Note: If the Frames panel is not open, click **Window** and then click **Frames**.*

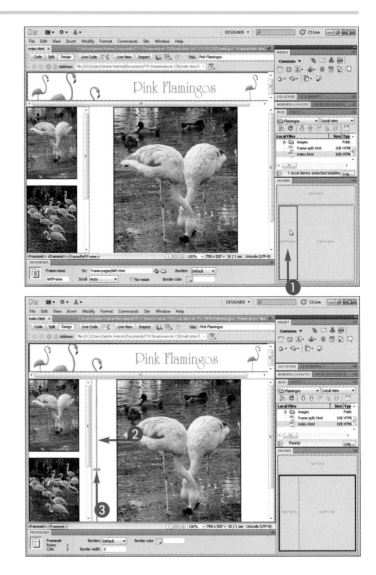

2 Click the border of the frame.

3 Drag to adjust the size.

The column adjusts to the specified width.

Set Frame Attributes

1 Click the frame that you want to change in the Frames panel.

● The Frame attributes are displayed in the Properties inspector.

● Click here to expand the Properties inspector.

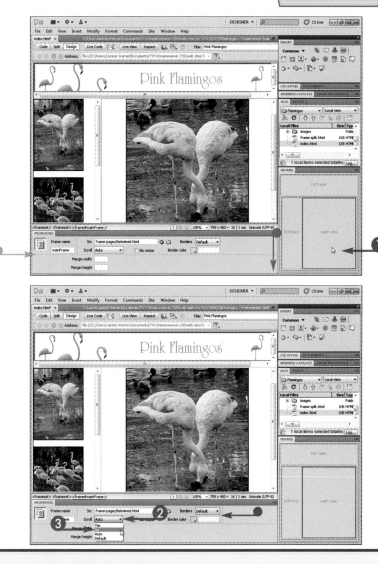

2 Click ▾.

3 Click a Scroll attribute.

The frame scroll bar changes, based on the option that you selected.

● You can also adjust the attributes for the border color and visibility in the Properties inspector.

 TIPS

Is there a shortcut for changing the dimensions of frames?

Yes. You can click and drag a frame border to quickly adjust the dimensions of a frame. When you select the border of a frame, its attributes are displayed in the Properties inspector.

Why would I want to change scrolling options?

When the content in a frame exceeds the dimensions of a Web browser window, you should include a scroll bar so that visitors can view all your content. If you set the Scroll attribute to **Yes** in the Properties inspector, the scroll bar is always visible. If you set it to **Auto**, a scroll bar appears only when needed.

Add Content to a Frame

You can insert text, images, and other content into a frame just as you would in an unframed page. You can also link existing pages into a frameset.

Open an Existing File in a Frameset

1. Click to position ▷ in the frame where you want to open an existing document.

2. Click **File**.

3. Click **Open in Frame**.

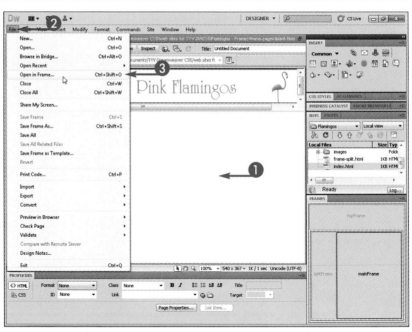

The Select HTML File dialog box appears.

4. Click ▾ and select a folder.

5. Click the file that you want to open in the frame.

6. Click **OK**.

- The selected page appears in the frame area.

- If the content extends beyond the frame, scroll bars automatically appear.

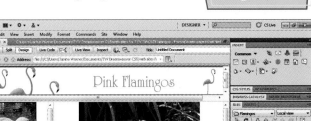

Add Text to a Frame

1 Click inside the frame where you want to add text.

2 Type the text.

Add Other Content to a Frame

- You can add images, `div` tags, or other elements by clicking the corresponding button, such as the Insert Images button () or the Insert Div button (📰) from the Common Insert panel.

TIPS

Can I link a frame to a page on the Web?

Yes. You can link to an external Web page address by using the **Link** field in the Properties inspector. However, unlike other pages, you must specify the target frame where you want the page to open. To create targeted links, see the section "Create a Link to a Frame."

Can I add as much content as I want to a frame page?

Yes. A frame page is just like any other page. You can add as much text, and as many images and multimedia files, as you want. However, if you have a small frame, you can have better design results by limiting the text within that frame page to fit the small space.

Delete a Frame

You can delete existing frames to change, simplify, or expand a design.

If you have saved the page displayed in the frame before you delete it, the HTML file is not deleted even though the frame is removed.

① Position ⌀ on the border of the frame that you want to delete (⌀ changes to ⌀).

② Click and drag the border to the edge of the window.

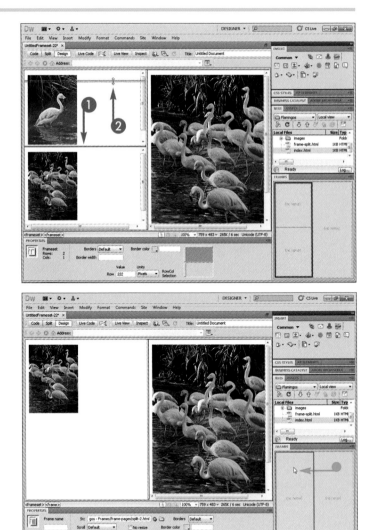

Dreamweaver deletes the frame.

● The deleted frame is also removed from the Frames panel.

If the Frames panel is not open, you can click **Window** and then click **Frames** to display it.

Name a Frame

Before you can target links in one frame to open in another frame, you need to ensure that all your frames have names. You use frame names to identify where the linked page should open in the frameset. Frame names are visible in the Frames panel.

This is Fred and Sarah, two good frames of mine.

Fred | Sarah

Frame 1 | Frame 2

Name a Frame

Note: If the Frames panel is not open, you can click **Window** and then click **Frames** to display it.

1. Click the frame that you want to name in the Frames panel.

2. Type a name for the frame.

   You can rename any frame by deleting the name in the Properties inspector and then typing in a new name.

3. Press Enter (Return).

● The new name of the frame appears in the Frames panel and the Properties inspector.

Create a Link to a Frame

You can create links in one frame that open a page in another frame. This is a common technique for navigation rows and other links that you want to continue to display when the linked page opens. For more information about creating links, see Chapter 7, "Creating Hyperlinks."

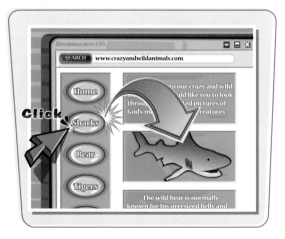

1 Click the text or image that you want to turn into a link.

2 Click 🖿 in the Properties inspector.

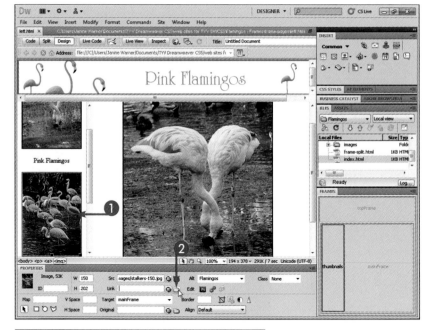

The Select File dialog box opens.

3 Click ▼ and select the folder containing the page to which you want to link.

4 Click the file.

5 Click **OK**.

6 Click the **Target** ▾.

7 Click the name of the frame where you want the target file to open.

● Dreamweaver automatically names frames when they are created. Frame names are visible in the Frames panel.

8 Click 🖳 and select a Web browser to preview the page.

Note: For more information about previewing a page in a Web browser, see Chapter 2, "Setting Up Your Web Site."

The page opens in the Web browser that you selected.

● When you click the link, the destination page opens inside the targeted frame.

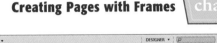
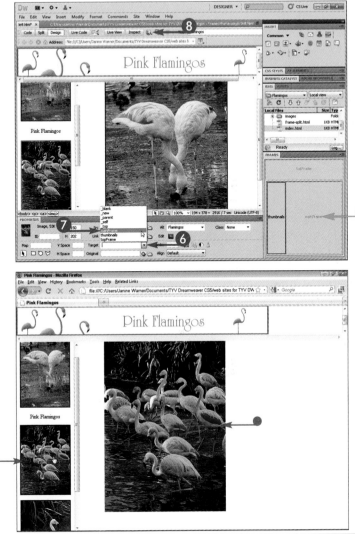

TIPS

How do I create a link that opens a new page, outside of the frameset?

When you target a link, you can click **_blank** from the **Link** drop-down menu in the Properties inspector, instead of a frame name, to open the linked page in its own new browser window. This action takes the user out of the frameset and is especially recommended when linking to another Web site.

Can I target a link to another Web site?

Yes. You can create a link to another Web site from a framed page by entering the URL in the **Link** field in the Properties inspector. However, use this feature with care. Many Web site owners consider it bad form (or worse) to display their Web pages within the frames on your Web site. Also, framing other Web sites can be confusing to visitors.

Format Frame Borders

You can modify the appearance of your frame borders to make them complement your design. One way is to specify the color and width of your borders. You can also turn them off so that they are not visible when the frameset is displayed in a Web browser.

Set the Border Color and Width

1 Click the corner of an outside frame border in the Frames panel to select the entire frameset.

2 Click the **Borders** ▼.

3 Click **Yes** or **Default** to turn on borders.

4 Type a border width in pixels.

5 Click the **Border color** ■ (↖ changes to ✐).

6 Click a color.

● The frame border appears at the specified settings.

You can override the frameset settings at the individual frame level if you want to change the settings to alter the border size or color of a single frame.

● To do so, click the corresponding frame area in the Frames panel to select that individual frame. Then change the settings in the Properties inspector.

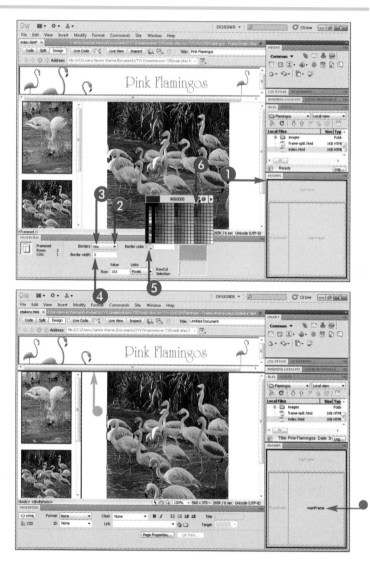

Turn Off Borders

1 Click the corner of an outside frame border in the Frames panel to select the entire frameset.

2 Click the **Borders** ▼.

3 Click **No**.

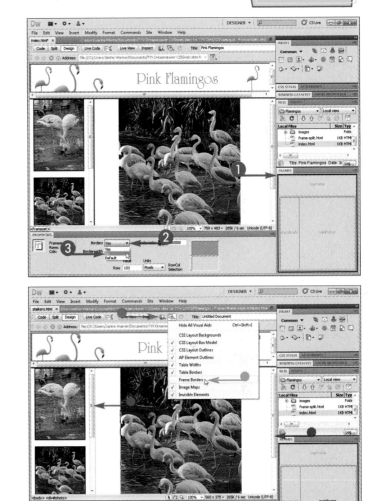

● The frame border is removed and will not be displayed in a Web browser.

● A gray border may still be visible in Dreamweaver if **Frame Borders** is selected on the Visual Aids menu.

● Scroll bars will be displayed unless turned off.

Links open in the targeted frame, even with borders turned off.

● You can click 🖳 and select a Web browser to preview the page.

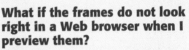

TIPS

Why would I want to make my frame borders invisible?

Turning borders off can disguise the fact that you are using frames in the first place. If you want to further disguise your frames, you can set the pages inside your frames to the same background color. To change background colors, see Chapter 6, "Working with Images and Multimedia."

What if the frames do not look right in a Web browser when I preview them?

Because pages can be displayed differently in different Web browsers than in Dreamweaver, you may want to make some adjustments to your frames after previewing them. If you find that the content is not exactly where you want it or if there are other problems with your frames, then simply return to Dreamweaver, click and drag to adjust the frame borders, and make any necessary adjustments to your content.

Control Scroll Bars in Frames

You can control whether scroll bars appear in your frames. Although hiding scroll bars enables you to have more control over the presentation of your Web site, it can also prevent the display of some of your text, images, or other content if they take up more room than is available in a browser window.

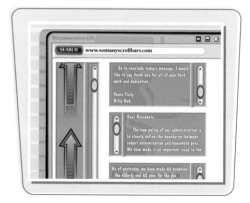

① Click the frame in the Frames panel to select it.

② Click the **Scroll** ▼.

③ Click a Scroll setting.

You can click **Yes** to keep scroll bars on, **No** to turn scroll bars off, or **Auto** to keep scroll bars on when necessary.

Note: In most Web browsers, Default and Auto settings have the same result.

● The frame appears with the new setting.

In this example, scroll bars are turned off in the main frame.

Note: Turning scroll bars off will prevent visitors to your site from being able to scroll to view the entire frame if the content exceeds the browser window.

Control Resizing in Frames

By default, most browsers allow users to resize frames by clicking and dragging frame borders.

You can prevent users from resizing the frames of a Web site. However, depending on the size of their monitor, this may make it more difficult for them to view all your content.

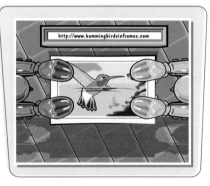

Control Resizing in Frames

1 In the Frames panel, click the frame to select it.

2 Click the **No resize** check box to remove the check mark if one is visible (☑ changes to ☐).

3 Click ⬛ and select a Web browser to preview the page.

Note: *For more information about previewing a page in a Web browser, see Chapter 2.*

● The browser allows the user to resize the frame.

When you select the **No resize** option, the browser prevents the user from resizing the frame.

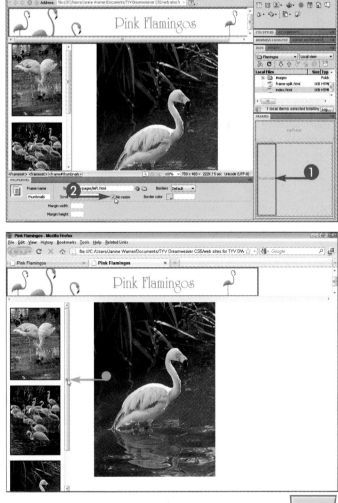

CHAPTER

10

Creating Web-Based Forms

You can make it easy for your Web site visitors to send you information by creating forms on your Web pages. This chapter shows you how to create forms with different types of fields, buttons, and menus.

Introducing Forms

You can add forms to your Web site to make it more interactive, thus allowing viewers to enter and submit information to you through your Web pages.

Note: In order for a form to function, you need to have a script on your Web server to process the form information. Contact your Web hosting service to learn more about the unique requirements of your Web server and if it offers scripts you can use to process forms. Most form scripts are written in a programming language such as Perl, PHP, ASP.NET, or Java.

Create a Form

You can use Dreamweaver to construct a form by inserting text fields, drop-down menus, check boxes, and other interactive elements into your page. You can also enter the Web address of a form handler, or script, in Dreamweaver so that the information can be processed. Visitors to your Web page fill out the form and send the information to the script on your server by clicking a Submit button.

Process Form Information

Form handlers, or *scripts,* are programs that process form information or execute an action, such as forwarding the contents of a form to an email address. Although many ready-made form handlers are available for free on the Web, they generally require some customization and special installation on your Web server. Your Web-hosting company may have forms available for you to use with your site. You can often find them by searching your hosting company's Web site or by calling tech support.

Define a Form Area

You set up a form on your Web page by first creating a form container. The form container defines the area of the form. You then place any text fields, menus, or other form elements inside the form container.

You associate the script, or form handler, on your Web server by selecting the form container and typing the name in the Properties inspector.

Define a Form Area

1 Click where you want to insert your form.

2 Click **Insert**.

3 Click **Form**.

4 Click **Form**.

● A red box appears, indicating that the form container is set up. To build the form, add elements inside the box.

5 Type the form address, using the name of the script and its location on your Web server.

6 Click ▼.

7 Click either **POST** or **GET**.

Note: Use the command required by your script, or form handler.

The form area is ready for you to insert form elements.

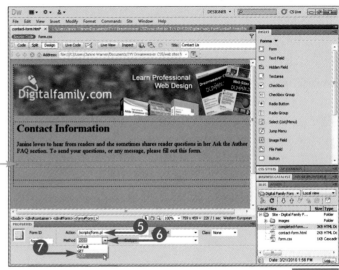

Add a Text Field to a Form

You can add a text field to enable viewers to submit text through your form. Text fields are probably the most common form element, enabling users to enter names, addresses, brief answers to questions, and other short pieces of text.

Add a Text Field to a Form

1 Click inside the form container where you want to insert the text field.

2 Click ▼.

3 Click **Forms**.

4 Click the **Text Field** button (▣) on the Forms Insert panel.

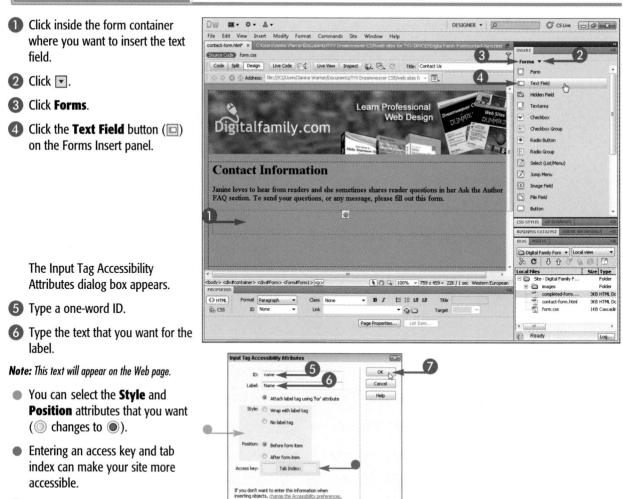

The Input Tag Accessibility Attributes dialog box appears.

5 Type a one-word ID.

6 Type the text that you want for the label.

Note: This text will appear on the Web page.

● You can select the **Style** and **Position** attributes that you want (◯ changes to ◉).

● Entering an access key and tab index can make your site more accessible.

7 Click **OK**.

- A text field appears.

- Your label text appears.

- You can click **Multi line** if you want more than one line available for text (⊚ changes to ⊙).

- You can change the assigned ID of the text field.

⑧ Type an initial value for the text field.

⑨ Type a character width to change the size of the text box.

- You can type a maximum number of characters to limit what a user can enter.

- The initial value appears in the text field.

- The width of the text field changes based on the value that you entered in the **Char Width** field.

⑩ Click and drag to select the label text.

⑪ Select any of the label formatting options in the Properties inspector.

- Dreamweaver applies the formatting to the label text.

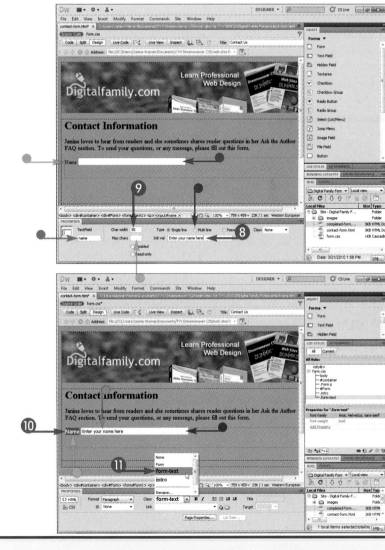

Can I define the style of text that appears in the text field?

By default, the browser determines what style of text appears in form fields. It is not possible to format this type of text with plain HTML. You can use style sheets to manipulate the way the text in the form fields appears. You can find more information about style sheets in Chapter 12, "Creating and Applying Cascading Style Sheets."

Can I create a text field with multiple lines?

Yes. You can create a text field and use the Properties inspector options to make it a field with multiple lines. You can also create a text area, which has multiple lines by default. You can insert a text area just as you insert a text field, except that you begin by clicking the Textarea button (📄) in the Forms Insert panel.

Add a Check Box to a Form

Check boxes enable you to present multiple options in a form and make it easy for a user to select one, several, or none of the options.

1. Click inside the form container where you want to insert the check box.

2. Click ▼.

3. Click **Forms**.

4. Click the **Checkbox** button (☑) on the Forms Insert panel.

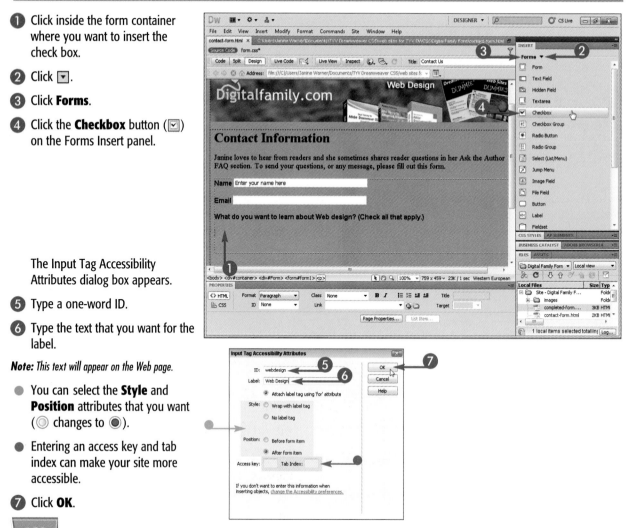

The Input Tag Accessibility Attributes dialog box appears.

5. Type a one-word ID.

6. Type the text that you want for the label.

Note: This text will appear on the Web page.

- You can select the **Style** and **Position** attributes that you want (◯ changes to ◉).

- Entering an access key and tab index can make your site more accessible.

7. Click **OK**.

● The check box and label appear on the page.

⑧ Repeat steps **1** to **7** until you have the number of check boxes that you want on your form.

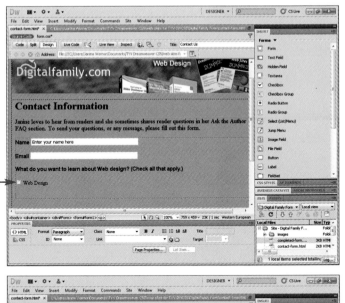

⑨ Click a check box to select it.

⑩ Click an **Initial state** option (◉ changes to ◉).

● You can specify other attributes, such as the class, ID, or checked value.

● You can click to select the other check boxes, one at a time, and specify the attributes of each separately.

● You can format the label text using the Properties inspector.

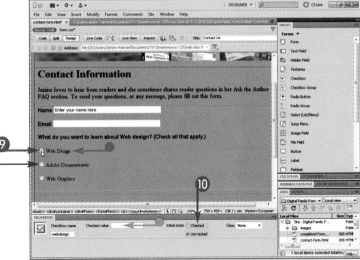

 TIPS

When should I use check boxes?

Check boxes are ideal when you want visitors to be able to select more than one option. Keep in mind that you may want to include the message "Check all that apply."

When should I use radio buttons?

When you want visitors to select only one option from a list of two or more options, radio buttons are the best choice. Radio buttons are designed so that it is not possible to select more than one option.

Add a Radio Button to a Form

You can allow visitors to select one of several options by adding a set of radio buttons to your form. With radio buttons, a user cannot select more than one option from a set.

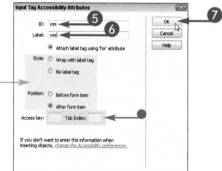

Add a Radio Button to a Form

1 Click inside the form container where you want to insert a radio button.

2 Click ▾.

3 Click **Forms**.

4 Click the **Radio Button** button (▣) on the Forms Insert panel.

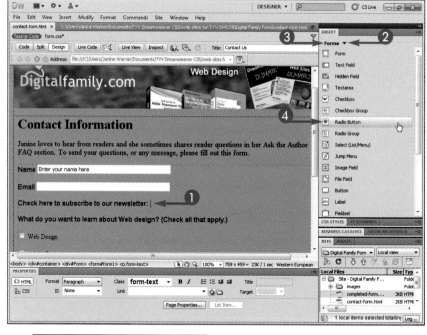

The Input Tag Accessibility Attributes dialog box appears.

5 Type a one-word ID.

6 Type a label.

Note: This text will appear on the Web page.

● You can select the **Style** and **Position** attributes that you want (◎ changes to ◉).

● Entering an access key and tab index can make your site more accessible.

7 Click **OK**.

● A radio button and a label appear on the page.

⑧ Repeat steps **1** to **7** until you have the number of radio buttons that you want on your form.

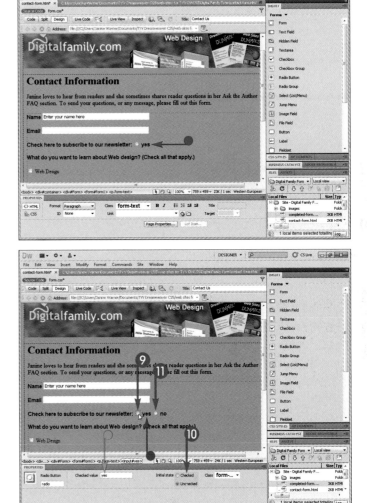

⑨ Click a radio button.

⑩ Click to select an **Initial state** option (◎ changes to ◉).

● You can specify other attributes, such as the checked value, ID, and class.

⑪ Click to select the other radio buttons one at a time and specify attributes for each individually.

● You can format the label text using the Properties inspector.

TIPS

What happens if I want visitors to select multiple options?

If you want your users to be able to select multiple options, radio buttons are not your best choice. If you want to allow your users to select multiple options and to be able to deselect an option after it is selected, your best choice is to use check boxes instead of radio buttons.

Are there alternatives to using check boxes or radio buttons?

Yes, there are alternatives such as menus and lists. Instead of using check boxes, you can use multiselect lists so that users can select more than one item from a list. You can also replace a radio button with a menu that allows only one choice from the list.

Add a List/Menu to a Form

List/menus enable users to choose from a predefined list of choices. List/menus, sometimes called *drop-down boxes,* are similar to check boxes in that users can choose one or more options.

① Click inside the form container where you want a menu or list.

② Click ▼.

③ Click **Forms**.

④ Click the **List/Menu** button (▤) on the Forms Insert panel.

The Input Tag Accessibility Attributes dialog box appears.

⑤ Type a one-word ID.

⑥ Type a label.

Note: This text will appear on the Web page.

● You can select the **Style** and **Position** attributes that you want (◎ changes to ◉).

● Entering an access key and tab index can make your site more accessible.

⑦ Click **OK**.

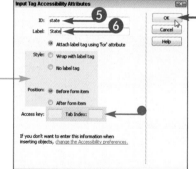

A blank menu appears in your form.

⑧ Click the menu to select it.

⑨ Click **List Values**.

The List Values dialog box appears.

⑩ Type an item label and a value for each menu item.

● You can click ⊞ or ⊟ to add or delete entries.

● You can select an item and click ▲ or ▼ to reposition the item in the list.

⑪ Click **OK**.

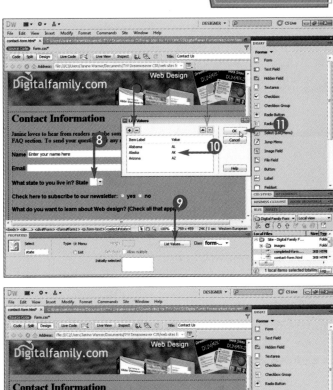

The entered values appear in the list box.

⑫ Click the item that you want to appear preselected when the page loads.

Dreamweaver applies your specifications to the menu.

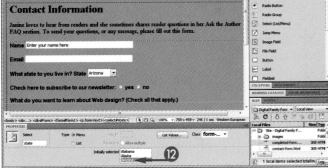

What determines the height and width of a menu or list?

The widest item determines the width of your menu or list. To change the width of the menu, you can change the length of your item descriptions. You can set the height greater than 1 so that visitors to your site can see more of your list items.

Can I choose more than one item from a menu?

You can select only one item from a menu because of its design. If you want more than one selection, use a list by clicking **List** as the type in the Properties inspector and set it to allow multiple selections.

Add a Button to a Form

You can use a form button for many things, but its most common use is to add a Submit button at the end of a form. You need a Submit button to enable users to send the information that they have entered in the form to the specified script, or form handler. You can also add a Reset button to clear the contents of a form.

Add a Submit Button

1 Click inside the form container where you want to add the Submit button.

2 Click ⏷.

3 Click **Forms**.

4 Click the **Button** button (▢) in the Forms Insert panel.

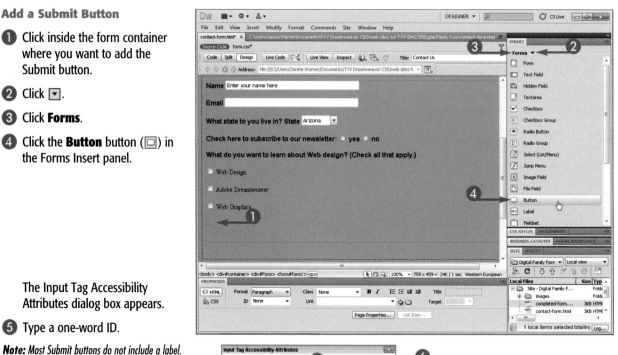

The Input Tag Accessibility Attributes dialog box appears.

5 Type a one-word ID.

Note: Most Submit buttons do not include a label.

● You can select the **Style** and **Position** attributes that you want (◎ changes to ◉).

● Entering an access key and tab index can make your site more accessible.

6 Click **OK**.

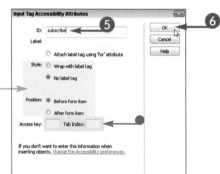

A Submit button appears in the form.

7 Click the button to select it.

8 Type a value for the button.

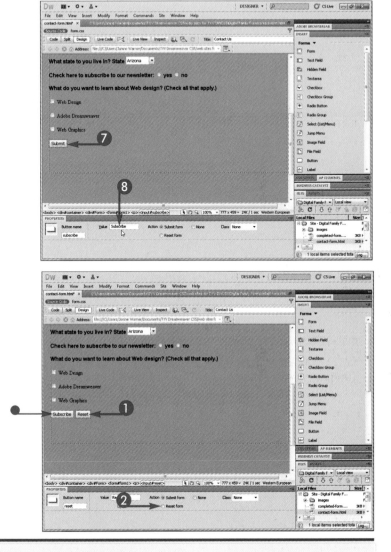

● The text on the button changes from **Submit** to the value that you entered.

Add a Reset Button

1 Repeat steps **1** to **8**, using a different ID in step **5**, such as **Reset**.

2 Click **Reset form** in the Properties inspector (◎ changes to ◉).

Why would I add a Reset button to a form on a Web page?
Including a Reset button is a common practice on the Web. Reset buttons make it easy for visitors to your site to clear the contents of a form if they have made an error and want to redo the form.

CHAPTER

11

Using Library Items and Templates

You can save time by storing frequently used Web page elements as library items. You can create sites even more efficiently by saving complete page layouts as templates. This chapter shows you how to quickly create consistent page designs with sections that can be updated automatically using Dreamweaver's template and library features.

Introducing Library Items and Templates

With library items and templates, you can avoid repetitive work by storing copies of page elements and layouts that you frequently use. You can access the library items and templates that you create through the Assets panel.

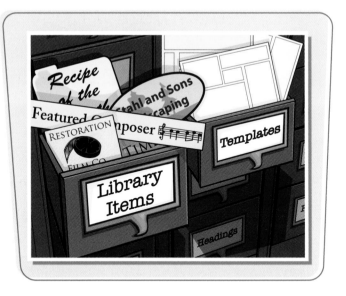

Library Items

You can define parts of your Web pages that are repeated in your Web site as library items. This saves you time because whenever you need a library item, you can just insert it from the Assets panel instead of re-creating it. If you make changes to a library item, Dreamweaver automatically updates all instances of the item across your Web site. Good candidates for library items include advertising banners, company slogans, copyright messages, and any other feature that appears many times across your Web site.

Templates

You can define entire Web pages as templates and then save them to use later when you build new pages. Templates can also help you maintain a consistent page design throughout a Web site. When you make changes to a template, Dreamweaver automatically updates all the pages in your Web site that were created from that template. The ability to make global updates to common areas of a template, such as a navigation bar, makes it faster to make changes to a site.

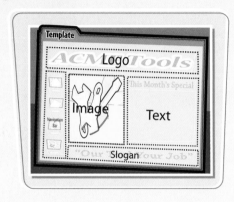

View Library Items and Templates

You can access the library items and templates in a Web site through the Assets panel. You can also insert items by dragging them from the Assets panel onto a Web page.

Note: **You must define a site in Dreamweaver before you can use these features. The site-definition process is covered in Chapter 2, "Setting Up Your Web Site."**

View Library Items and Templates

View the Library

1 Click **Window**.

2 Click **Assets**.

● The Assets panel opens.

3 Click the Library button (📖).

● The Library window opens in the Assets panel.

View Templates

1 Click **Window**.

2 Click **Assets**.

● The Assets panel opens.

3 Click the Template button (📄).

● The Templates window opens in the Assets panel.

Create a Library Item

You can save text, links, images, and other elements as library items. A copyright message is a great example of content that works well as a library item. This is because you can save a collection of images, text, and links that you can quickly insert into other pages without having to re-create them.

If you edit a library item, Dreamweaver automatically updates each instance of the item throughout your Web site.

Create a Library Item

1 Click and drag to select an element or collection of elements that you want to define as a library item.

Note: Before you can use the library item feature in Dreamweaver, you must first set up and define your local site. To set up a local site, see Chapter 2.

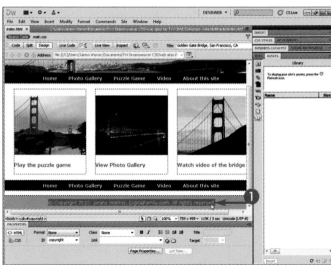

2 Click **Modify**.

3 Click **Library**.

4 Click **Add Object to Library**.

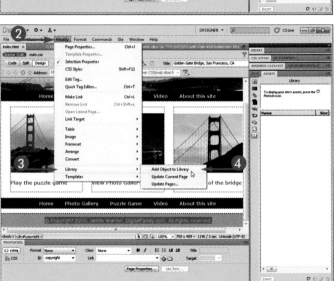

● A new, untitled library item appears in the Library window.

⑤ Type a name for the library item.

⑥ Press **Enter** (**Return**).

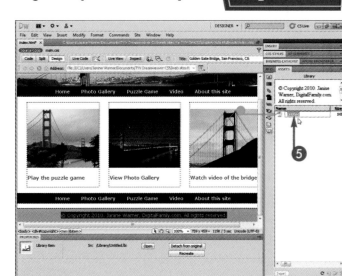

● The named library item appears in the Assets panel.

Note: *Defining an element as a library item prevents you from editing it in the Document window.*

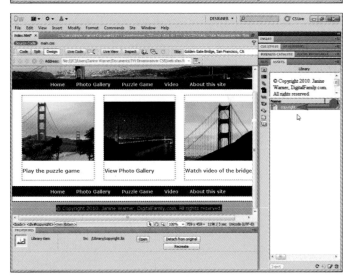

TIPS

What page elements should I make into library items?

Anything that appears multiple times in a Web site is a good candidate to become a library item. These elements include navigation menus, contact information, and disclaimers. Any element that appears in the body of an HTML document, including text, images, tables, forms, layers, and multimedia, may be defined as a library item.

Can I use multiple library items on the same HTML page?

There is no limit to the number of library items that you can use on a page. For example, you can create a library item for the logo at the top of the page and another for the copyright at the bottom.

Insert a Library Item

You can insert any library item onto a page to avoid having to re-create it. This ensures that the element is identical to other instances of that library item and that it can be easily updated if you make changes to the library item later.

Insert a Library Item

1 Click **Window**.

2 Click **Assets**.

The Assets panel opens.

● If the Library window is not open in the Assets panel, you can click ▣ to view it.

3 Click the name of the library item.

● A preview of the library item appears at the top of the Library window.

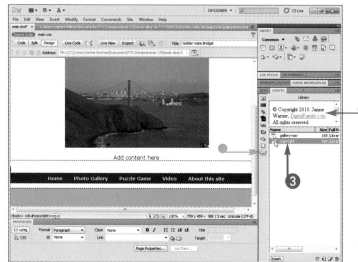

④ Click and drag the library item onto the page where you want it to appear.

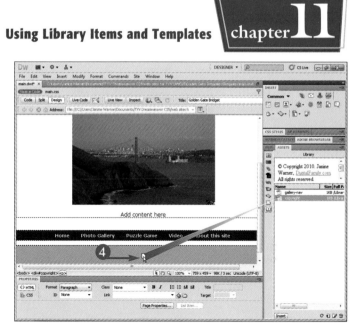

● Dreamweaver inserts the library item in the Document window.

How do I edit a library item that has been inserted into a page?

Instances of library items in your page are locked and cannot be edited within the page. To edit a library item, you must either edit the original version of that item from the library or detach the library item from the library to edit it within the page. However, if you detach the library item from the library, the item is no longer a part of the library, and it is not updated when you change the library item.

Can I make an element a library item after I have used it on a few pages?

Yes. You can save any item to the library at any time. If you want to make sure that all instances of the item are attached to the library item, simply open any pages where you have already applied the item, delete it, and then insert it from the library.

Edit and Update a Library Item on Your Pages

You can edit a library item and then automatically update all the pages in your Web site that feature that item. This ability to make global changes can help you save time when updating or redesigning a Web site.

Edit and Update a Library Item on Your Pages

1 Double-click the library item.

The library item opens in a new window.

2 Edit any element in the library item.

You can add or delete text, insert images, and make any other edits to a library item that you can make to a Web page.

Note: *In this example, the year 2010 is changed to 2011 in the copyright library item.*

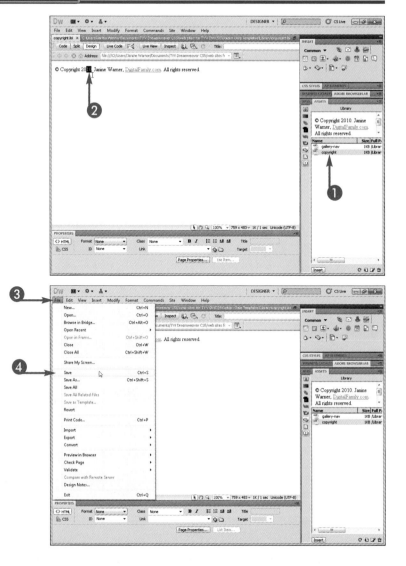

3 Click **File**.

4 Click **Save**.

You can also save the page with the key command Ctrl + S (⌘ + S).

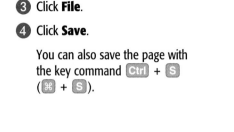

The Update Library Items dialog box appears, asking if you want to update all instances of the library item in the site.

⑤ Click **Update**.

The Update Pages dialog box appears, showing the progress of the updates.

⑥ After Dreamweaver updates the site, click **Close**.

All pages in which the library item appears are updated.

● The changes are also made to the stored library item and are visible in the Assets panel.

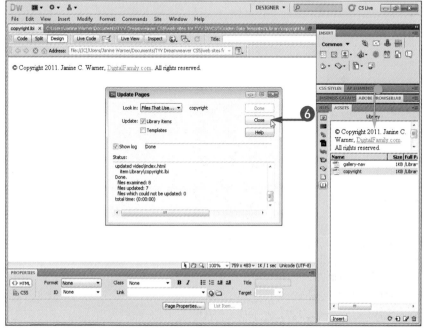

TIPS

What do my pages look like after I have edited a library item and updated my Web site?

When you edit a library item and choose to update any instances of the library item that are already inserted into your Web pages, all those instances are replaced with the edited versions. By using the library feature, you can make a change to a single library item and have multiple Web pages updated automatically.

Can I undo an update to a library item?

Technically, no. When you update pages with the library feature, the Undo command does not undo all the instances of these changes. However, you can go back to the Assets panel, open the library item, change it back to the way it was, and then apply those changes to all the pages again.

Detach Library Content for Editing

You can detach an inserted library item from the original stored library item and then edit it as you would any other element on a Web page. If you detach a library item, you can no longer make automatic updates when you change the original stored library item.

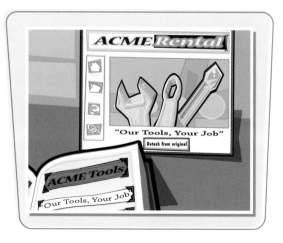

① Click to select the library item that you want to edit independently.

② Click **Detach from original**.

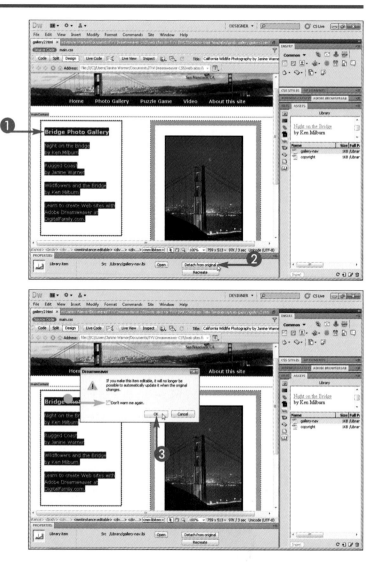

A warning dialog box appears.

● You can prevent the warning from appearing each time that you perform this action by clicking **Don't warn me again** (☐ changes to ☑).

③ Click **OK**.

The element is no longer a library item and has no distinctive highlighting.

④ Click where you want to edit the library item and make any changes that you want.

● You can add, delete, and format text. In this example, the text in the last section is edited.

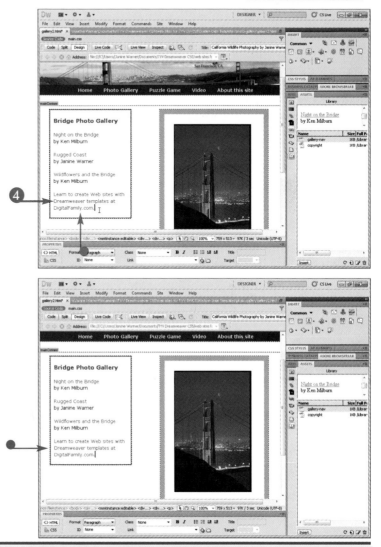

● Dreamweaver applies the editing only to the page you are working on.

Note: *Editing a detached library item has no effect on library items that are used on other pages.*

When would I use the Detach from Original option?

This option is useful when you want to create an element in a page that will be similar to an element that you have saved as a library item. For example, if you use a copyright line that includes the photographer's name on every page of a 20-page photo gallery and then you decide to add one page with a photo taken by a different photographer, you could detach the library item so that you could change only that instance of the copyright line.

Can I reattach a library item?

Not exactly, but you can always reinsert a library item into a page and then delete the unattached library item. As a result, any changes that you make to the stored version are applied to the newly inserted version. Inserting a library item again may be faster than making the updates manually.

Create a Template

Templates are one of the most powerful and time-saving features in Dreamweaver because they enable you to create page designs that can be reused over and over again. Templates can also help you create more consistent designs for your pages.

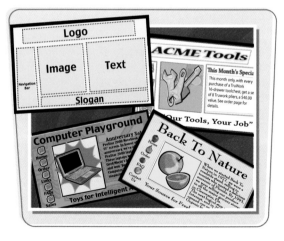

Create a Template

Note: *To create templates for your Web pages, you must already have defined a local Web site. To set up a local Web site, see Chapter 2.*

1 Click **File**.

2 Click **New**.

The New Document dialog box appears.

3 Click **Blank Template**.

4 Click **HTML template**.

You can choose another template type if you are working on a site that uses another technology.

5 Click a Layout option.

6 Click **Create**.

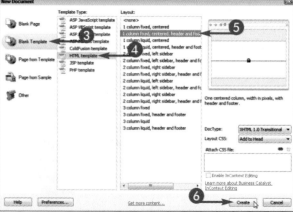

⑦ Design a new page as you would for any other Web page, using the features that you want for your template.

● You can add placeholder images and text to indicate where content is to be added to the pages created from the template.

⑧ Click **File**.

⑨ Click **Save**.

If a Dreamweaver error dialog box appears with the warning "This template doesn't have any editable regions," click OK.

The Save As Template dialog box appears.

⑩ Click ▾ and select your site name.

⑪ Type a name for the template.

⑫ Click **Save**.

New templates appear in the Templates window.

● If the Templates folder does not already exist, Dreamweaver automatically creates one, and it appears in the Files panel.

Note: *To make the template functional, define editable regions to modify content, as discussed in the next section, "Set an Editable Region in a Template."*

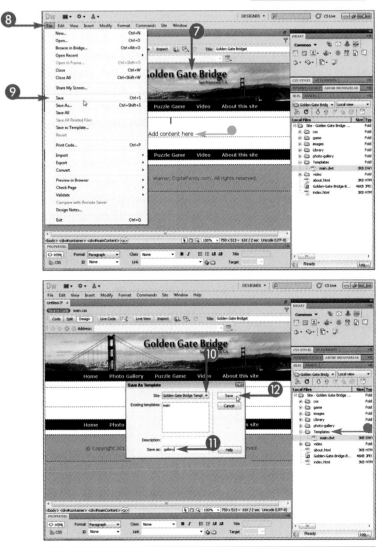

 TIPS

Can I create as many pages as I want from a template?

Yes. There is no limit to the number of pages that you can create from one template. In fact, the more pages that you plan to create using the same design, the more reason you have to save that design as a template, so it does not have to be re-created each time.

How do you edit a page that is created with a template?

After you create a new Web page from a template, you can change only the parts of the new page that are defined as editable. To change locked content, you must edit the original template file. For more information about creating editable regions in a template, see the following section, "Set an Editable Region in a Template."

Set an Editable Region in a Template

After you create a Web page template, you must define which regions of the template are editable. When you create a page from the template, you can then edit these regions. Any areas of the template that are not set as editable cannot be changed in any pages that you create from the template.

Set an Editable Region in a Template

① Click **Window**.

② Click **Files**.

The Files panel appears.

③ Click the **Templates** + (+ turns to –).

④ Double-click a template name to open it.

You can also open a template by double-clicking the template name in the Assets panel.

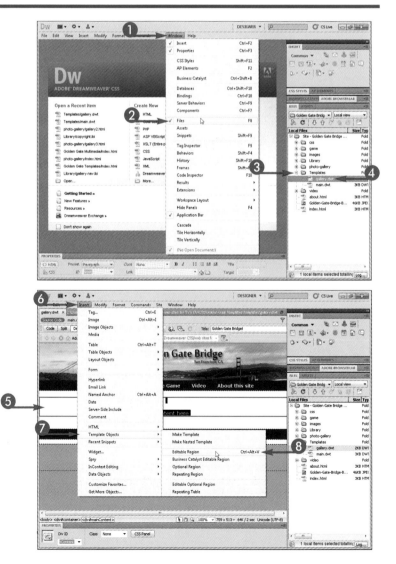

The template opens in the work area.

⑤ Click to select an image or other element that you want to define as editable.

Note: In this example, I selected a `div` *tag.*

⑥ Click **Insert**.

⑦ Click **Template Objects**.

⑧ Click **Editable Region**.

The New Editable Region dialog box appears.

9 Type a name for the editable region that distinguishes it from other editable regions on the page.

Note: You cannot use special characters, such as punctuation marks, in a template name.

10 Click **OK**.

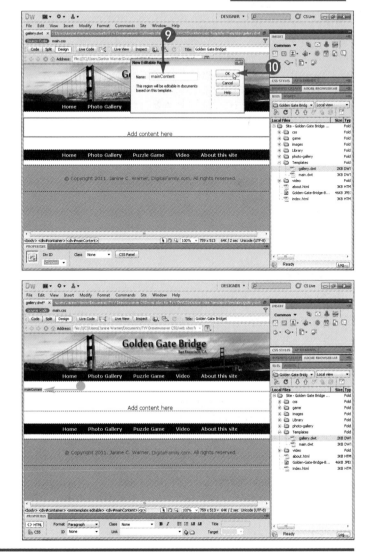

● A light-blue box indicates the editable region, and a tab shows the region name.

11 Repeat steps **5** to **10** for all the regions on the page that you want to be editable.

TIPS

What parts of a template should be defined as editable?

You should define as editable any part of your template that you want to change from page to page. This can include headlines, stories, images, and captions. In contrast, you should lock site navigation, disclaimers, and copyright information, which should be the same on all pages.

Can I use library items in my template pages?

Yes, you can use library items in templates. This is useful when you want to insert an item on pages that are made from the template. When you edit them, the library items are updated in the actual templates — and then in all of the pages that are created from those templates.

Create a Page from a Template

You can create a new Web page based on a template that you have already defined. This step saves you from having to rebuild all the generic elements that appear on many of your pages.

① Click **File**.

② Click **New**.

The New Document dialog box appears.

③ Click **Page from Template**.

④ Click the name of the Web site.

⑤ Click the template.

● A preview of the template appears.

⑥ Click **Create**.

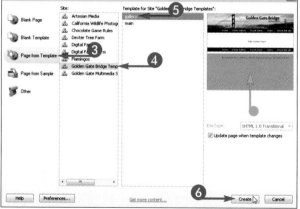

Dreamweaver generates a new page from the template.

● The editable regions have blue labels and are surrounded by blue boxes.

⑦ Insert images as needed into the editable regions.

⑧ Type content as needed in the editable regions.

Note: Only editable areas can be altered in a page created from a template.

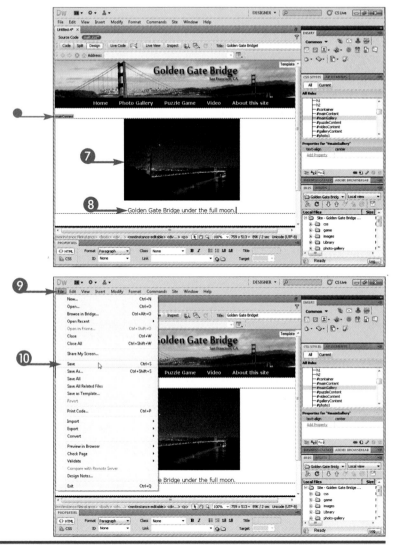

⑨ Click **File**.

⑩ Click **Save**.

Dreamweaver saves the new page, based on the template.

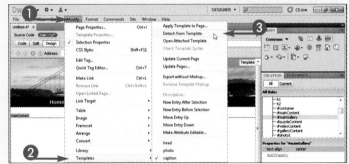

TIP

How do I detach a page from a template?

① Click **Modify**.

② Click **Templates**.

③ Click **Detach from Template**.

The page becomes a regular document with previously locked regions now fully editable. Edits to the original template no longer update the page.

Edit a Template to Update Web Pages Created with It

When you make updates to a template file, Dreamweaver gives you the option to automatically update all the pages that are created by the template. This enables you to make global changes to your Web site design in seconds.

Edit a Template to Update Web Pages Created with It

① Click **Window**.

② Click **Files**.

The Files panel appears.

③ Click the **Templates** + (+ turns to –).

④ Double-click the template name to open it.

You can also open a template by double-clicking the template name in the Assets panel.

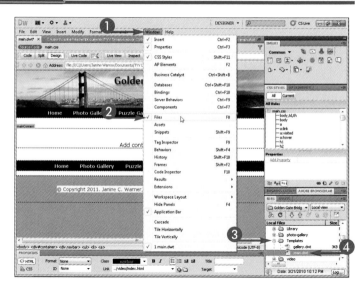

⑤ Click the area of the template that is not an editable region that you want to change.

Note: *Only locked regions of a template can be used to make updates to pages created from the template.*

⑥ Make the edits that you want.

Note: *In this example, the text of a navigation menu link is edited.*

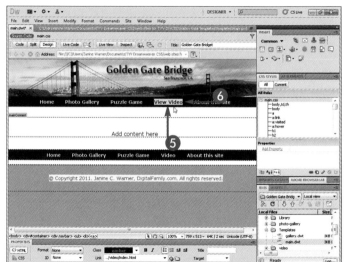

7 Press Ctrl + S (⌘ + S) to save the page.

The Update Template Files dialog box appears, listing all files based on the selected template that will be updated.

8 Click **Update**.

The Update Pages dialog box appears.

9 Click **Show log** (☐ changes to ☑).

● The results of the update process appear in the Status pane.

10 After Dreamweaver updates the Web site, click **Close**.

All the pages that use the template are updated to reflect the changes.

TIPS

How does Dreamweaver store page templates?

Dreamweaver stores page templates in a folder called *Templates* inside the local site folder. You can open the templates by clicking **File** and then clicking **Open**. In the Open dialog box, click ▼ and click the **Templates** folder. You can click a template file to select it. You can also open templates from inside the Assets panel.

What are editable attributes?

Editable attributes enable you to change the attributes of an element in the Properties inspector. For example, you can change image attributes, such as alternative text, alignment, or size. To use this feature, select an element, such as an image, click **Modify**, then click **Templates**, and then click **Make Attribute Editable**.

CHAPTER 12

Creating and Applying Cascading Style Sheets

This chapter shows you how to use cascading style sheets (CSS) to create and apply formatting. Cascading style sheets can save you a lot of tedious formatting time, especially if you format big Web sites.

Introducing Cascading Style Sheets

You can apply many different types of formatting to your Web pages with style sheets, also known as *cascading style sheets*, or *CSS*.

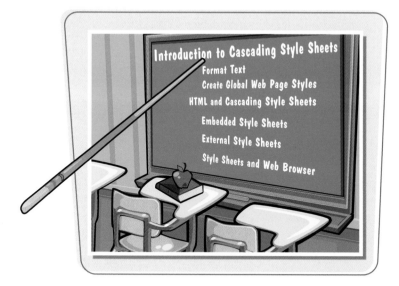

Format Text

CSS enables you to create as many different style sheets as you want. You can then use them to format text by applying multiple formatting options at once, such as the font face, size, and color.

Create Page Layouts

You can use styles for more than just formatting text. You can create styles to align and position elements on a Web page. Using styles in this way, you can create complex page designs that display well on small and large computer screens. You can find more instructions for creating page layouts in Chapter 13, "Designing a Web Site with CSS."

Cascading Style Sheet Selectors

Dreamweaver includes four different style selector types: the tag selector to redefine existing HTML tags, the class selector to create new styles that can be applied to any element on a Web page, the ID selector to create styles that can be used only once per page, and the compound selector, which can be used to combine style definitions.

Internal Style Sheets

A style sheet saved within the HTML code of a Web page is called an *internal style sheet*. Internal style sheet rules apply only to the page in which they are included.

External Style Sheets

When you want your styles to apply to multiple pages on your Web site, you must save them in a separate file called an *external style sheet.* You can attach the same external style sheet to any or all of the pages in a Web site.

Style Sheets and Web Browsers

Some older Web browsers do not support style sheet standards, and different Web browsers display style sheets differently. Always test pages that use style sheets in different browsers to ensure that the content is displayed as you intend it to for all your visitors.

Edit Styles with the Properties Inspector

Dreamweaver CS5 includes a CSS mode in the Properties inspector. You can use the HTML settings to format and style tags and use the CSS settings to create and edit CSS styles.

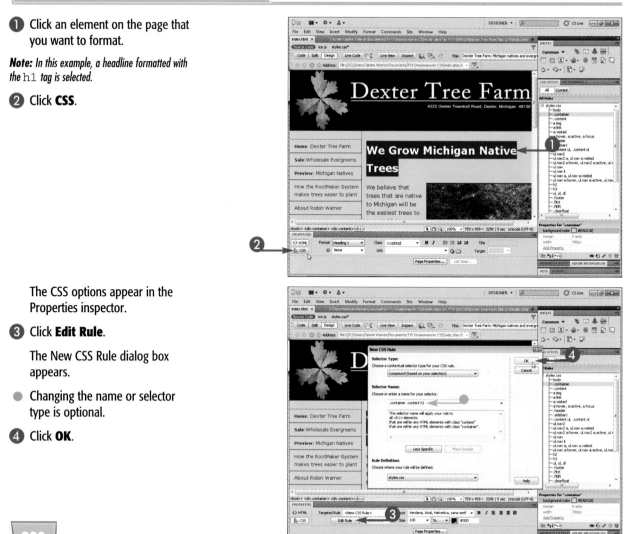

Unedited Style   Edited Style

① Click an element on the page that you want to format.

Note: *In this example, a headline formatted with the* h1 *tag is selected.*

② Click **CSS**.

The CSS options appear in the Properties inspector.

③ Click **Edit Rule**.

The New CSS Rule dialog box appears.

● Changing the name or selector type is optional.

④ Click **OK**.

The CSS Rule Definition dialog box appears.

5 Click a style category.

6 Select the style settings that you want.

● You can click **Apply** to see a preview of the style.

7 Click **OK**.

8 Click the **CSS Styles** tab.

● You can also click **Window** and then click **CSS Styles** to open the CSS Styles panel.

● The CSS Styles panel opens, displaying the new style.

● Any content that is formatted with the same tag is automatically updated.

Note: *In this example, the font face and size are changed for the text formatted with the Heading 1 tag.*

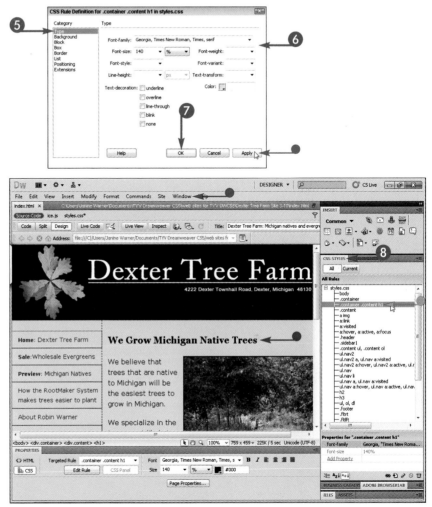

TIPS

Why are compound styles created in the Properties inspector?

When you edit an element such as a selection of text using the Properties inspector, Dreamweaver automatically creates compound styles if the selected element is contained in an existing style. When you select h1 text, for example, Dreamweaver includes any related styles and creates a compound style that looks like this: #container #mainContent h1. This style for an h1 tag created as a compound style will apply to text formatted with the h1 tag only if it is contained within elements, usually div tags, styled with #container and #mainContent on the page.

Can the same styles be edited in the Properties inspector and the CSS Styles panel?

Yes. You can create and edit styles using both the CSS Styles panel and the Properties inspector, and styles created or edited in one place will automatically be updated in the other. The main difference is that the CSS Styles panel includes more features for editing and reviewing styles, and the Properties inspector, in HTML mode, can also be used to apply class and ID styles.

Create a Class Style

You can create class styles that can be used to format text and other elements on a Web page without affecting HTML tags. You can then apply those styles to any elements on your Web page, much like you would apply an HTML tag.

1 Click **Format**.

2 Click **CSS Styles**.

3 Click **New**.

The New CSS Rule dialog box appears.

4 Click ▼ and select **Class**.

5 Type a name for the class style.

Note: Class style names must begin with a period (.). Dreamweaver adds one automatically.

6 Click ▼ and select an internal or external style sheet option.

Note: Choose **This document only** to add the style to an internal style sheet or choose any existing style sheet, such as the styles.css file used in this example. You can also create a new style sheet as you create the style by choosing **New Style Sheet File**. See the section "Create an External Style Sheet" to learn more.

7 Click **OK**.

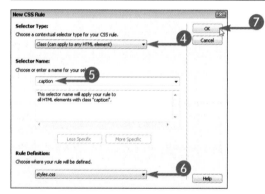

202

The CSS Rule Definition dialog box appears.

8 Click a style category.

9 Select the style settings that you want.

Note: *In this example, text style options are used to change the font face, size, and weight (to make the font bold).*

10 Click **OK**.

11 Click the **CSS Styles** tab.

● You can also click **Window** and then click **CSS Styles**.

● The CSS Styles panel opens, displaying the new class style.

You can apply the class style to new or existing content using the Properties inspector.

Note: *To apply a new class style, see the following section, "Apply a Class Style."*

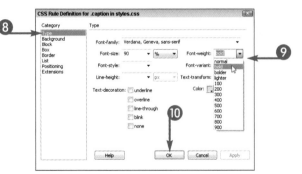

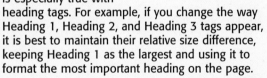

What are the best uses of class styles?

The class selector is great for creating styles that you may want to use multiple times on the same page — for example, a text style for captions or a formatting style that you can use to align elements on a page. Class styles can also be used in combination with other styles.

Is it better to customize an HTML tag or create my own class styles?

One of the benefits of redefining existing HTML tags is that you can take advantage of recognized styles and hierarchies. This is especially true with heading tags. For example, if you change the way Heading 1, Heading 2, and Heading 3 tags appear, it is best to maintain their relative size difference, keeping Heading 1 as the largest and using it to format the most important heading on the page.

Apply a Class Style

You can apply a class style to any element on your Web page. Class styles enable you to change color, font, size, alignment, and other characteristics. You can use the same class style multiple times on the same page.

Apply a Class Style to Text

Note: *To create a new custom style, see the previous section, "Create a Class Style."*

① Click and drag to select the text to which you want to apply a style.

② In the Properties inspector, click HTML.

③ Click the **Class** ▾.

④ Click the name of the style that you want to apply to the text.

● Dreamweaver applies the style.

Note: *In this example, a class style named .caption is applied to the text under the photo.*

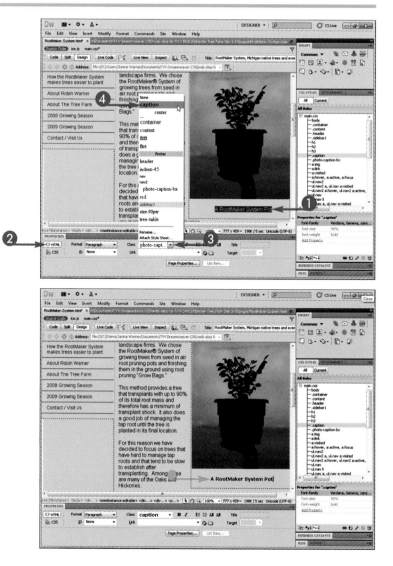

Apply a Class Style to an Image

Note: To create a new custom style, see the previous section, "Create a Class Style."

1 Click the image to select it.

2 In the Properties inspector, click the **Class** ▼.

3 Click the name of the style.

● Dreamweaver applies the new style sheet to the image in the Document window.

Note: In this example, a class style named .fltrt is applied to the image, which aligns the image to the right and adds 8 pixels of margin space to the left side of the image.

 TIPS

What are some other options that I can use to define the formatting for text with a style sheet?

With style sheets, you can specify a numeric value for font weight. This enables you to apply varying degrees of boldness, instead of just a single boldness setting as with HTML. You can also define type size in absolute units, such as pixels, points, picas, inches, centimeters, or millimeters, or in relative units, such as ems, exes, or percentage.

Can I create as many styles as I want?

Yes. However, one of the goals of style sheets is to help you work more efficiently, so you should try to create styles that are as efficient as possible in the way they contain formatting options.

Edit a Style

You can edit style sheet definitions. You can then automatically apply the changes across all the text or other elements to which you have applied the style on your Web page or Web site.

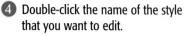

① Click **Window**.

② Click **CSS Styles**.

● The CSS Styles panel opens.

③ Click **All** to display all the available styles.

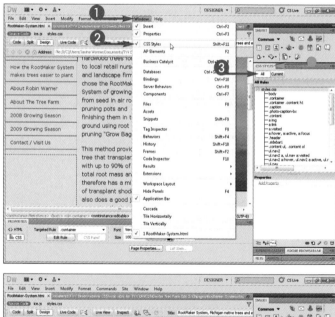

④ Double-click the name of the style that you want to edit.

The CSS Rule Definition dialog box opens.

⑤ Click a style category.

⑥ Select the new style settings that you want.

Note: *In this example, the font color is changed.*

⑦ Click **OK**.

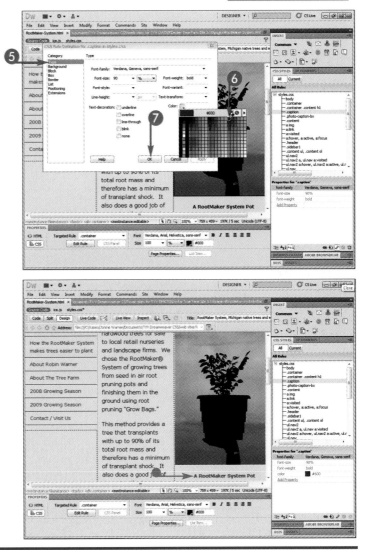

Dreamweaver saves the style sheet changes and automatically applies them anywhere that you have used the style.

● In this example, the font color changes automatically in the text where the style has already been applied.

TIP

How many different kinds of styles are there?

You can create multiple kinds of style rules, but the main options are tag styles, class styles, ID styles, and compound styles. Tag styles are used to redefine HTML tags. Class styles are used to create new styles that can be applied to any element on a page and used multiple times. ID styles are commonly used with `<div>` tags to control the placement of elements on a page and create page layouts.

Customize an HTML Tag

You can customize the style that an existing HTML tag applies. This enables you to apply special formatting whenever you use that tag to format text. This is a quick, easy way to apply multiple style options with one HTML tag.

Not Customized <h1>

Customized <h1>

① Click **Format**.

② Click **CSS Styles**.

③ Click **New**.

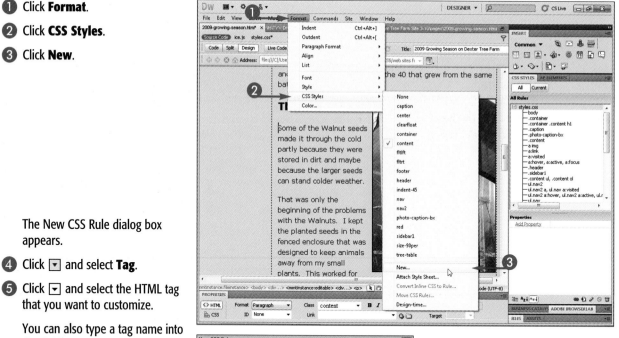

The New CSS Rule dialog box appears.

④ Click ▼ and select **Tag**.

⑤ Click ▼ and select the HTML tag that you want to customize.

You can also type a tag name into the field.

⑥ Click ▼ and select **This document only** or choose an external style sheet.

Note: To create style sheets for more than one document, see the section "Create an External Style Sheet."

⑦ Click **OK**.

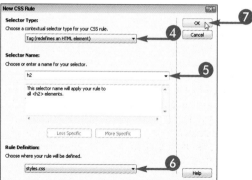

The CSS Rule Definition dialog box appears.

⑧ Click a style category.

⑨ Select the style settings that you want.

⑩ Click **OK**.

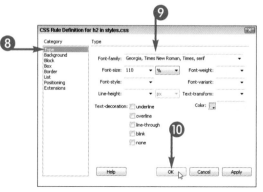

● Dreamweaver adds the new style to the CSS Styles panel.

● Any content that is formatted with the redefined tag is updated.

Note: In this example, the h2 tag is redefined to use a different font face and size.

● In this example, you can also apply the style by selecting content on the page and clicking **Heading 2** on the **Format** drop-down list.

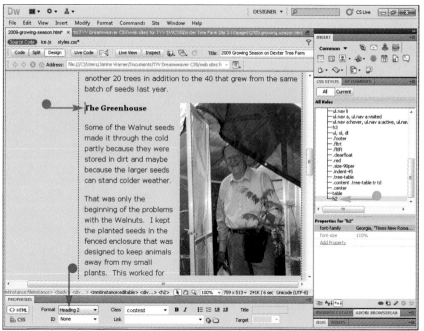

 TIPS

Why should I redefine an HTML tag?

When you redefine an HTML tag, you can apply more than one style to it. As a result, you have to use only one HTML tag instead of several to apply multiple formatting options. For example, you can add center alignment to all your Heading 1 tags to control the alignment of heading styles in one step. A special advantage of redefining HTML tags is that if a user's Web browser does not support style sheets, the HTML tag still provides its basic formatting.

Does redefining an HTML tag change the format of any content that uses that tag?

Yes. When you redefine an HTML tag, you change the tag's formatting effect anywhere that you use the tag. You can limit the change to the page that you are working on, or you can include it in an external style sheet and apply it to an entire site. If you do not want to alter the style of an existing HTML tag, you should create class style sheets instead of redefining HTML tags.

Change the Font Face

You can change the font style of your text in a variety of ways in Dreamweaver, but all of them require using CSS.

Dreamweaver CS5 added a CSS mode to the Properties inspector to make it easy to create style rules as you format text and other elements.

Change the Font Face

① Click and drag to select the text.

② Click **CSS** in the Properties inspector.

③ Click the **Font** ▾.

④ Click a font collection.

Note: Leave the **Targeted Rule** field set to *<New CSS Rule>*.

The New CSS Rule dialog box opens.

⑤ Type a name for the new style.

Note: Do not use spaces or special characters.

● If the selected text is already formatted with an HTML tag, Dreamweaver inserts the tag name into the Selector Name field.

Note: In this example, the headline is formatted with an h1 tag, which is recommended for the most important headline on the page.

⑥ Click **OK**.

● The text changes to the first font in the collection that is available on your hard drive.

The new style can be applied to additional elements by using the Properties inspector.

⑦ Click the **CSS Styles** tab.

⑧ Click the name of the new style rule.

⑨ Click ▼ and select a different font collection, if needed.

● The font face is changed.

 TIPS

How are fonts classified?
The two most common categories of fonts are serif and sans serif. Serif fonts are distinguished by the decorations, or *serifs,* that make the ends of their lines curly. Common serif fonts include Times New Roman, Palatino, and Garamond. Sans serif fonts lack these decorations and have straight edges. Common sans serif fonts include Arial, Verdana, and Helvetica.

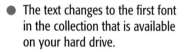

Why are there so few fonts available from the Font menu?
A font must be installed on the user's computer to be displayed in a Web browser. Dreamweaver's default list of fonts specifies the common typefaces that are available on most computers and alternative styles if the user does not have those fonts installed. If you want to use an unusual font, you should convert the text to a graphic.

Change the Font Size

You can change the size of your text by using the font size tag. Unlike the heading tags, when you apply the font size tag, Dreamweaver does not add a paragraph return.

① Click and drag to select the text.

② Click the **Targeted Rule** ▾.

③ Click the name of a style, such as the one created in the preceding section, "Change the Font Face."

Note: *If you have not yet created a style, you can choose <New CSS Rule>.*

④ Click the **Size** ▾.

⑤ Click a font size.

● The size of the text changes.

The CSS style rule changes to include the size setting.

You can change the color of text on all or part of your Web page. You should ensure that it is readable and complements the background.

1 Click and drag to select the text that you want to change.

2 Click the **Targeted Rule** ▾.

3 Click the name of a style.

Note: *If you have not yet created a style, you can choose* **<New CSS Rule>**.

4 Click the Color Swatch ▣.

The Color Palette appears.

5 Click a color.

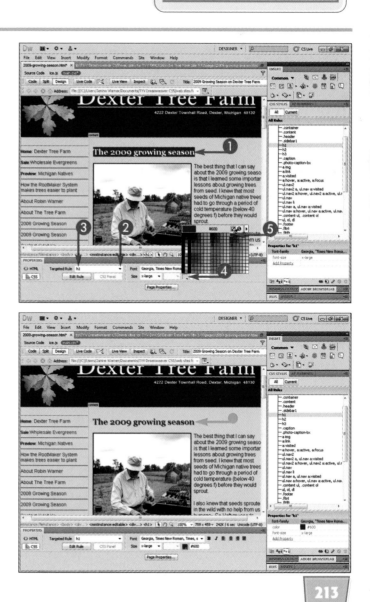

● The selected text appears in the new color.

The CSS style rule changes to include the color setting.

Change Font and Text Colors

You can change the font face, color, and size, as well as other formatting options for the entire page in the Page Properties dialog box.

① Click **Modify**.

② Click **Page Properties**.

● You can also click **Page Properties** in the Properties inspector.

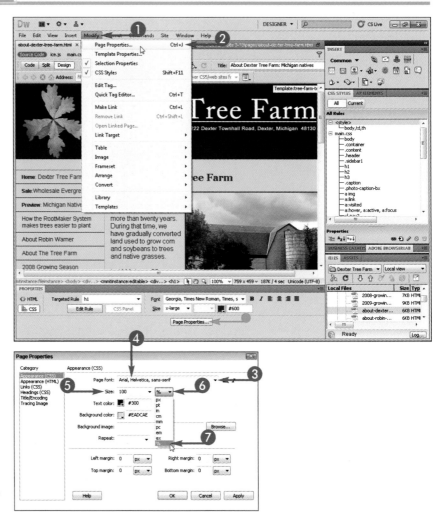

The Page Properties dialog box appears.

③ Click the **Page Font** ▾.

④ Click the font collection that you want.

⑤ Click the **Size** ▾ and choose a preset size or enter a number.

⑥ Click this ▾.

⑦ Click a font size option to select it.

8️⃣ Click the **Text Color** ▣.

The Color Palette appears.

9️⃣ Click the color that you want.

🔟 Click **Apply** to see the changes applied to the page.

1️⃣1️⃣ Click **OK** to save the changes and close the dialog box.

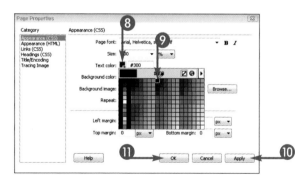

Your text appears in the new font, size, and color on your Web page.

● Dreamweaver creates the corresponding styles, and they appear in the CSS Styles panel.

What are the letter and number combinations that appear in the color fields of Dreamweaver?

HTML represents colors using six-digit codes called *hexadecimal codes*, or *hex codes*. These codes start with a pound sign (#) and are followed by a series of numbers that represent the amount of red, green, and blue used to create a particular color. Instead of ranging from 0 to 9, hex-code digits range from 0 to F, with A equal to 10, B equal to 11, and so on through to F, which is equal to 15. The first two digits in the hex code specify the amount of red in the selected color. The second two digits specify the amount of green, and the third two digits specify the amount of blue. When you select a color from a color picker, Dreamweaver automatically generates the corresponding hex code.

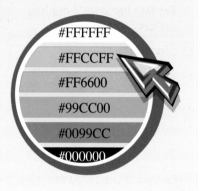

#FFFFFF
#FFCCFF
#FF6600
#99CC00
#0099CC
#000000

Create Styles with the Page Properties Dialog Box

You can use Dreamweaver's Page Properties dialog box to define pagewide styles, such as background colors, link styles, and text options.

When you define these options in the Page Properties dialog box, Dreamweaver automatically creates the corresponding styles and adds them to the Styles panel.

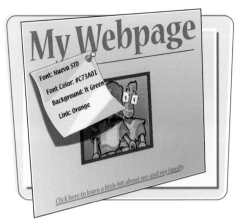

① Click **Page Properties** in the Properties inspector.

The Page Properties dialog box appears.

② Click **Appearance (CSS)**.

③ Select the font, size, color, and spacing that you want.

④ Set page margins to **0** to remove the default indent in the left and top margins of the display area.

⑤ Click **Apply**.

6 Click **Links (CSS)**.

7 Select the font, size, and link colors.

8 Click ▾ and select an underline style, such as **Never underline** to remove the underline style from all links on the page.

9 Click **OK**.

● Dreamweaver saves the corresponding styles in the Styles panel.

● Dreamweaver automatically applies the new style information to the page.

Note: *In this example, the background color for the entire page is changed.*

TIPS

What are some nontext-based features that I can implement with style sheets?

Probably the most exciting thing that you can do with style sheets is to position elements precisely on the page. Style sheets offer you freedom from traditional, and imprecise, layout methods, such as HTML tables. Style sheets often use the `<div>` tag, which defines an area on the page where you can position an element with alignment attributes. You can also position elements more precisely by specifying margin and padding settings.

Do all Web browsers support CSS in the same way?

No, unfortunately not all Web browsers support CSS in the same way, and some do not support styles at all. However, styles have come a long way in the last few years, and so have browsers. Although some visitors may not be able to see your designs as you intend if you use CSS, the vast majority of people surfing the Web these days have browsers that support CSS.

Create an External Style Sheet

External style sheets enable you to define a set of style sheet rules and then apply them to many different pages — even pages on different Web sites. This enables you to keep a consistent appearance across many pages and to streamline formatting and style updates.

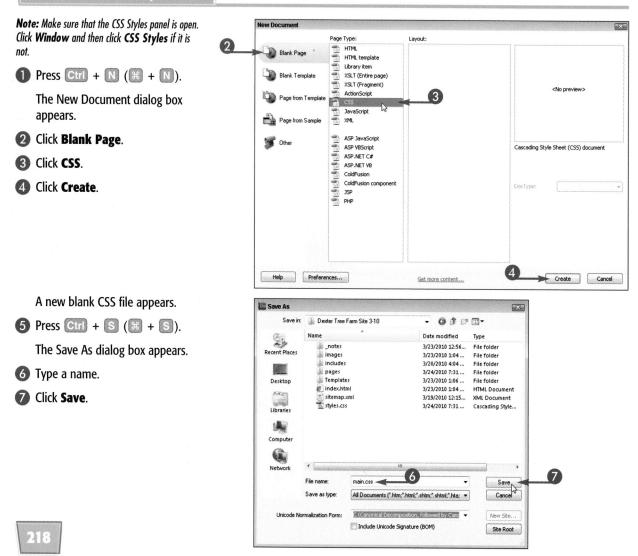

Create an External Style Sheet

Note: *Make sure that the CSS Styles panel is open. Click* **Window** *and then click* **CSS Styles** *if it is not.*

1 Press Ctrl + N (⌘ + N).

The New Document dialog box appears.

2 Click **Blank Page**.

3 Click **CSS**.

4 Click **Create**.

A new blank CSS file appears.

5 Press Ctrl + S (⌘ + S).

The Save As dialog box appears.

6 Type a name.

7 Click **Save**.

- The style sheet is displayed in the CSS Styles panel.
- The name of the style sheet appears in the Files panel.
8 Click ⊠ to close the external style sheet.

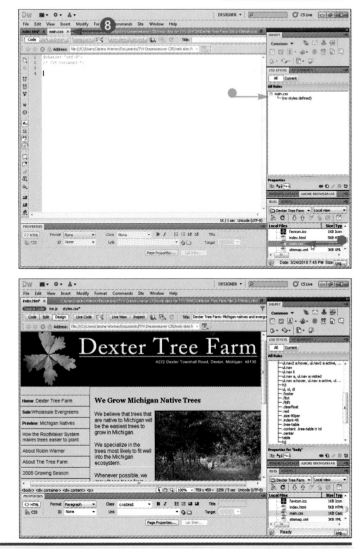

The style sheet closes.

If you have another document open in the background, it becomes visible in the workspace.

Note: *The external style sheet is created inside your local site folder. For this to work, you must have defined your site in Dreamweaver. To define a site and identify the local site folder, see Chapter 2, "Setting Up Your Web Site."*

 TIPS

How can I add more styles to an external style sheet?
When you create any new style, you have the option of selecting an existing style sheet from the **Rule Definition** field in the New CSS Rule dialog box. To create a class style, see the section "Create a Class Style." To customize an HTML tag, see the section "Customize an HTML Tag." When you define a new style in an external style, it is automatically added to the selected CSS file.

Is it possible to add new styles later?
Yes. You can add styles to an external style sheet at any point during production, even months after the site was first published. In addition, you can make changes or additions while you work on any page that is currently attached to an external style sheet, and those styles will become available on any page where the style sheet is attached.

Attach an External Style Sheet

After you have created a style sheet, you can attach it to any or all of the Web pages in your site. You can even attach multiple style sheets to the same page. After you attach an external style sheet to a page, all the style rules in the style sheet become available, and you can apply them to elements on the page just as you would apply styles from an internal style sheet.

① With the page to which you want to attach a style sheet open, click **Format**.

② Click **CSS Styles**.

③ Click **Attach Style Sheet**.

The Attach External Style Sheet dialog box appears.

④ Click **Browse**.

The Select Style Sheet File dialog box appears.

⑤ Click the name of the style sheet that you want to attach.

⑥ Click **OK**.

You are returned to the Attach External Style Sheet dialog box.

⑦ Click **OK**.

● The external style sheet is linked to the page, and the style sheet is displayed in the CSS Styles panel.

Any styles in the external style sheet are automatically applied to the page.

Note: *To apply styles to content in a document, see the section "Apply a Class Style."*

⑧ Click and drag to move a style from the page's internal style sheet to the external style sheet.

● You can move any or all of the styles from an internal style sheet to an external one.

● To delete a style or to remove a style sheet from a file, click to select it and press Del.

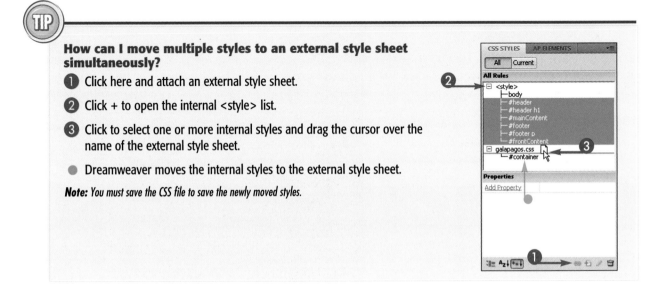

TIP

How can I move multiple styles to an external style sheet simultaneously?

① Click here and attach an external style sheet.

② Click + to open the internal <style> list.

③ Click to select one or more internal styles and drag the cursor over the name of the external style sheet.

● Dreamweaver moves the internal styles to the external style sheet.

Note: *You must save the CSS file to save the newly moved styles.*

Edit an External Style Sheet

You can include hundreds of styles in a single external sheet. This enables you to continue to add to the style sheet as your site grows and to change or add sections.

① Click **Window**.

② Click **CSS Styles**.

● The CSS Styles panel appears.

● You can click here and drag to expand the CSS Styles panel.

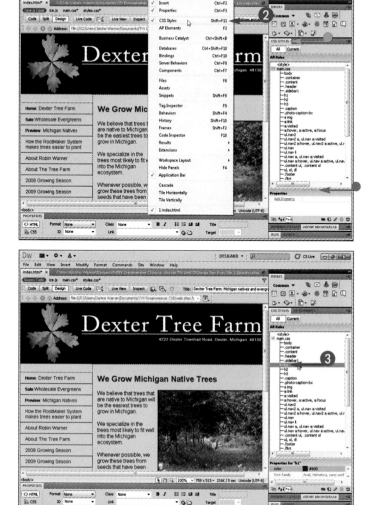

③ Double-click the name of the style that you want to modify.

The CSS Rule Definition dialog box appears.

④ Click a style category.

⑤ Select the style settings that you want.

● In this example, the font color is changed.

⑥ Click **OK**.

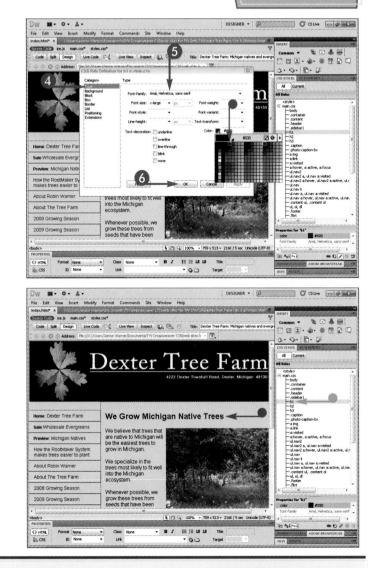

● Dreamweaver saves the new style definition in the external style sheet.

● The new style is automatically applied to any content formatted with that style on all pages to which the external style sheet is attached.

What problems can arise when I use CSS?

The benefits to using cascading style sheets are enormous, and they mostly outweigh the challenges that come with their implementation. However, because CSS does not display the same in all Web browsers, pages designed with CSS may not be displayed the same on all computers. You should always test your pages to make sure that you like the results in all the browsers that you expect your visitors to use. For the best results, redefine existing HTML tags when possible and create your page designs so that they will be readable and display well even if the styles are not supported.

Designing a Web Site with CSS

In addition to creating styles for text, you can use CSS to create styles that position and align elements on a page. Using styles with divs and other HTML tags, you can create complex layouts in Dreamweaver that meet today's Web standards.

Introducing CSS Layouts

You can use advanced Dreamweaver tools to create CSS layouts that are flexible, adapt well to different screen sizes and resolutions, and are accessible to all your site visitors.

The CSS Box Model

One of the most popular and recommended approaches to Web design today is the CSS Box model. By combining a series of HTML `div` tags with CSS styles, it is possible to create designs that are complex in their appearance but simple in their construction. One of the advantages of this model is that Web pages with CSS layouts display well on a variety of devices.

Alignment with Floats

Instead of using the familiar left and right alignment icons, the best approach to aligning images and other elements with CSS is to create styles that use floats. By floating elements to the right or left of a page, you can align them and cause any adjacent elements, such as text, to wrap around them.

Note the unusual migratory habits of the Northern Plains area shaved homonid over a range of territory. A male Sasquatch has been known to travel dozens of miles in a single day

Centering CSS Layouts

The Center attribute is no longer recommended in CSS, so how do you center a design? The trick is to set the margins on both the left and right of a div to "auto," or automatic. This causes a browser to automatically add the same amount of margin space to both sides of the element, effectively centering it on the page.

Dreamweaver's CSS Layouts

Dreamweaver includes a large collection of CSS layouts that are carefully designed and ready for you to use to create your own Web pages. Although you will need to edit the CSS styles to customize these layouts, they can give you a great head start and help you avoid some of the common layout challenges of CSS.

AP Div Basics

AP Divs are discrete blocks of content that you can precisely position on the page, make moveable by the user, and even make invisible. Most significantly, you can stack AP Divs on top of each other. AP Divs can contain any kind of content, including text, graphics, tables, and even other AP Divs. Unfortunately, layouts created completely with AP Divs are not very flexible and thus not well-suited to the many different displays in use on the Web. Use AP Divs sparingly and test to ensure that your pages work properly on a variety of screen sizes and Web browsers.

Nested AP Divs

AP Divs can contain nested AP Divs, which create areas of content that stay linked together on a page for better control during the production of Web pages. *Nested,* or child, AP Divs can inherit the properties of their parent divs, including visibility or invisibility. You can also nest AP Divs within divs that do not use absolute positioning.

Create a Web Page with a CSS Layout

Dreamweaver includes a collection of CSS layouts to make it easy to design pages using HTML `div` tags and styles. Creating a new page with a CSS layout is as easy as creating a new blank page — but with the advantage of already having many design elements in place.

Create a Web Page with a CSS Layout

1. Click **File**.

2. Click **New**.

The New Document dialog box opens.

3. Click **Blank Page**.

4. Click **HTML**.

5. Click a layout option.

6. Click **Create**.

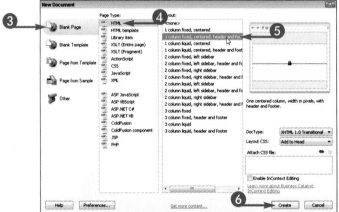

Dreamweaver creates a page with the selected layout.

⑦ Add a page title by changing the text here.

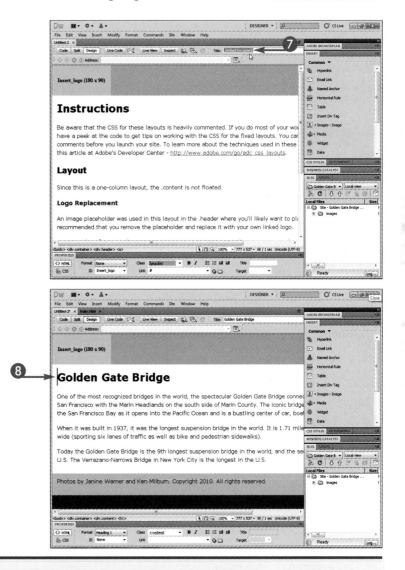

⑧ Replace the placeholder text in the layout with your own text.

⑨ Press Ctrl + S (⌘ + S) to save the page.

Note: *Never use spaces or special characters in the name of a Web page. Hyphens (–) and underscores (_) are okay.*

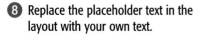

Can I create new styles for a CSS layout?

Yes. You can create and apply new styles in a CSS layout just as you would any other page in Dreamweaver. Dreamweaver's CSS layouts include a collection of styles needed to create the original design, but you can add as many styles as needed for formatting and layout.

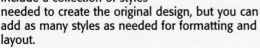

Can I save CSS layout styles to an external style sheet?

Yes. You can always move styles to an external style sheet. First, create a new CSS file, then attach it to the page, and finally click and drag the styles into the external style sheet in the CSS Styles panel. You can find more detailed instructions in the previous chapter "Creating and Applying Cascading Style Sheets."

You can edit the CSS layouts that are included in Dreamweaver. However, if you are not familiar with CSS, editing one of these page layouts can be confusing.

CSS layouts cannot be edited in the design area of Dreamweaver. You must change the styles in the CSS Styles panel to edit the layout.

Edit a CSS Layout

Note: If the CSS Styles panel is not open, click **Window** and then click **CSS Styles** to open it.

① Double-click the name of the style that you want to change.

Note: In this example, I selected the .footer style.

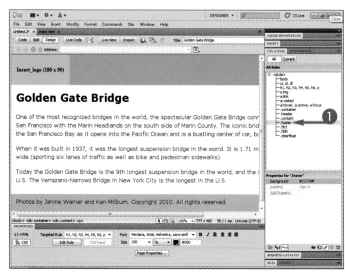

The CSS Rule Definition dialog box appears.

② Click a category.

③ Edit the style.

Note: In this example, the background color for the footer style is changed.

④ Click **OK**.

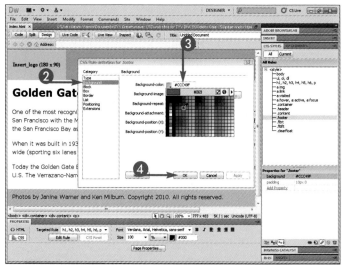

● The changes to the style are automatically applied in the workspace.

Note: In this example, the background color in the footer area changes.

● The style is updated in the CSS Styles panel, and the new style option is displayed in the panel's Properties pane.

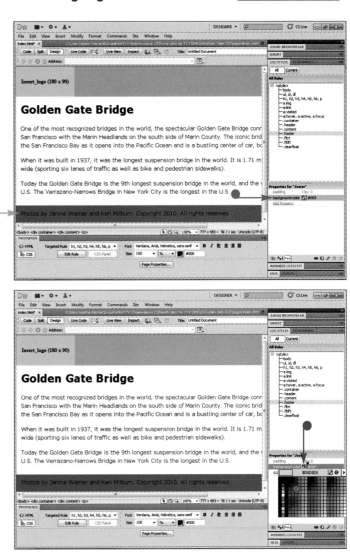

● You can also edit CSS styles in the CSS Styles Properties pane.

Note: In this example, the background color is selected, displaying the color swatches.

TIP

How do I know which style corresponds to each part of the layout?

To identify what style is controlling the design of any part of the page, place your cursor in the page where you want to change the style and look at the tag selector at the bottom of the design area (just above the Properties inspector). In the tag selector, you see all the tags that surround whatever you have selected in the design area. Another way to identify styles is to view the HTML source code. Choose the Split view and select some text or an image that is in an area of the page that you want to edit. Then look in the code to see what style is applied to your selection.

To begin with,

Cafeteria Black
Red 18 pt.

Add an Image to the Header

All of Dreamweaver's CSS layouts include an area at the top of the page for a header. You can add images or text to the header area.

If you want to add only text, delete the image placeholder and type text as you would anywhere else on the page.

Add an Image to the Header

*Note: If the CSS Styles panel is not open, click **Window** and then click **CSS Styles** to open it.*

1. Double-click to select the image placeholder in the banner.

2. Click ⏷ and select the folder that contains the image.

3. Click the name of the image.

4. Click **OK**.

   If the Image Tag Accessibility Attributes dialog box appears, enter a description and click **OK**.

   The image appears in the header area of the layout.

   To delete any text on the page, click and drag to select it and press Del.

5. Click to select the image.

6. Delete the text in the **Alt** field and type your own description of the image that you inserted.

7. Press Enter (Return).

   The text in the Alt field is saved and will be visible in a browser if the image is not displayed.

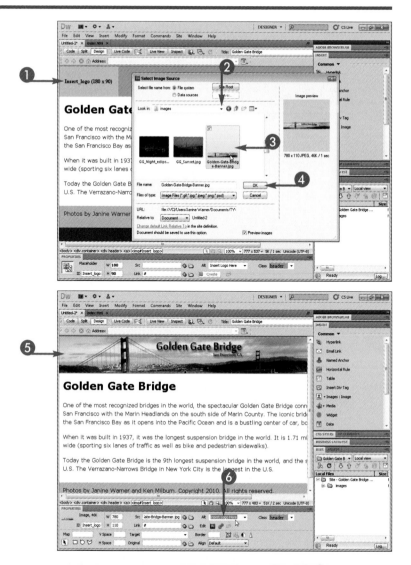

⑧ Click the **CSS Styles** tab.

Note: *Alternatively, you can click **Window** and then click **CSS Styles** to open the CSS Styles panel.*

⑨ Double-click the name of the .header class style.

The CSS Rule Definition dialog box appears.

⑩ Click **Background**.

⑪ Click ◼ and change or delete the background color.

Note: *If you delete the background color of the header, its background color will change to the color of the page.*

⑫ Click **OK**.

The color behind the banner image is changed.

TIP

Can I change the width of a CSS layout?

Yes. The width setting for the CSS layouts in Dreamweaver is controlled by the class style named `.container`. Select the `.container` style name in the CSS Styles panel and then change the width setting to alter the width of the entire CSS layout. You can find more detailed instructions in the section "Change the Dimensions of a CSS Layout" later in this chapter.

Add Images to a CSS Layout

You can insert images into a CSS layout just as you would insert them into any other page in Dreamweaver. After you have inserted an image, you can format and align it using CSS.

Add Images to a CSS Layout

*Note: If the CSS Styles panel is not open, click Window and then click **CSS Styles** to open it.*

1 Click to place ⩥ where you want to add an image.

2 Click **Window**.

3 Click **Insert**.

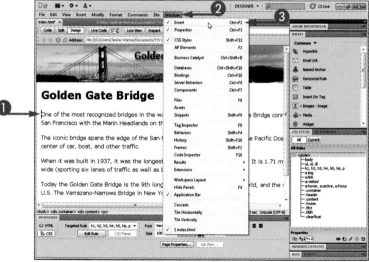

4 Click the **Images** 🖼.

The Select Image Source dialog box appears.

5 Click ▾ and select the folder that contains the image.

6 Click the name of the image.

7 Click **OK**.

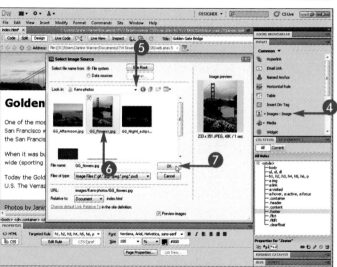

The Image Tag Accessibility Attributes dialog box appears.

8 Type a description of the image.

● A long description URL is optional.

9 Click **OK**.

● The image appears in the layout.

To remove or replace the Latin text included in CSS layouts, select the text and press **Del**. Then type to enter the new text or use copy and paste.

Can I change the background color of the page?

Yes, you can change the background color of the entire page in a CSS layout just like you would change the background color on any page — by using the Page Properties dialog box. Click **Window** and then click **Page Properties** to open the dialog box. Choose the **Background** category and use the **Background Color** field to select a color.

Can I change the background color of only a section of the page?

You can change or add color to any section of the page by creating a rule that assigns a color to the style that controls that part of the page. For example, to change the background color of an individual `div` tag in the design, you have to edit the corresponding CSS style. To learn more, see the section "Edit a CSS Layout."

Using Floats to Align Elements

You can use CSS styles to align images and other elements on a Web page. Many designers create class styles that float elements to the right and left, an ideal way to wrap text around an image.

Many of Dreamweaver's CSS layouts include class styles for floats with the names fltrt **to float elements to the right and** fltlft **to float elements to the left.**

Using Floats to Align Elements

Align to the Left

Note: *If the CSS Styles panel is not open, click* **Window** *and then click* **CSS Styles** *to open it.*

① Click to select an image or other element that you want to align.

② Click the **Class** ▾.

③ Click **fltlft**.

The image or other element aligns to the left, and any text on the page wraps up around it.

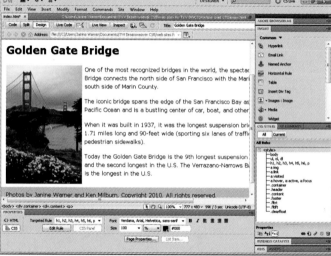

Align to the Right

1. Click to select an image or other element that you want to align.

2. Click the **Class** ▾.

3. Click **fltrt**.

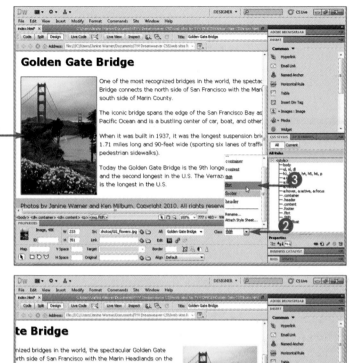

The image aligns to the right, and any text on the page wraps up around it on the left.

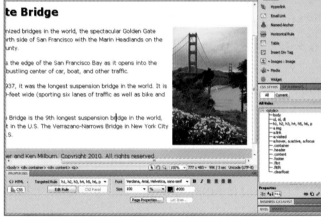

TIP

Can I create my own styles to float elements to the right or left?
Yes, you can use floats in many different kinds of styles. To create a style to float elements to the left or right, create a new style and in the **Box** category, choose **Right** or **Left** from the **Float** drop-down list. You can combine many rules in one style.

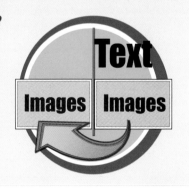

Change the Dimensions of a CSS Layout

You can change the overall width of any page design. You can also change the width of sections of a design, such as a sidebar, by changing the width settings in the corresponding CSS style.

All the CSS layouts in Dreamweaver CS5 include a class style named `.container` that controls the width of the entire design area.

Note: If the CSS Styles panel is not open, click *Window* and then click **CSS Styles** to open it.

1 Double-click the **.container** style in the CSS Styles panel.

The CSS Rule Definition dialog box appears.

2 Click **Box**.

The Box category's options are displayed.

③ Type a width setting.

Note: In this example, the width is being changed from 960 pixels to 780 pixels.

④ Click **OK**.

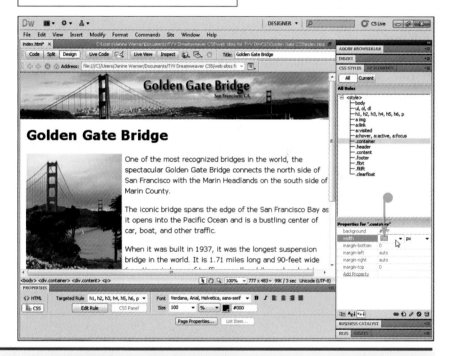

The width of the page design changes to the width that you specified.

● You can also change the width in the CSS Styles panel's Properties pane.

TIPS

Why can I not drag the edge of a column to change the size?

You cannot change a CSS layout by simply clicking and dragging the border of a `div` tag. To edit the width or height of any of the divs in a Dreamweaver CSS layout, you have to edit the corresponding CSS style. In most CSS layouts on the Web, that style is named `container` or `wrapper`.

How wide should I make my Web page layout ?

As a general rule, you should create Web page layouts that are 780 pixels wide or 960 pixels wide, depending on the size of the monitors you expect your visitors to use. Most Web designers today create layouts that are 960 pixels wide because most computers today have monitors that support at least a 1024 x 768 screen resolution. Limit the size to 960 even though it will be displayed on a 1024 screen to leave room for the browser scroll bars.

Change the Color of a Headline

You can change the color of a headline by creating a new style to control the appearance of the headline or by editing an existing style that affects the headline.

In this section, you create a new style to change the headline color.

Note: *If the CSS Styles panel is not open, click* **Window** *and then click* **CSS Styles** *to open it.*

1. Click and drag to select the headline.

2. Click the New CSS Rule button (image).

The New CSS Rule dialog box appears.

● The selector type is already selected.

Note: *Do not change this unless you want to create a different kind of style.*

● The name of the new style is already entered into the **Selector Name** field.

3. Click **OK**.

240

The CSS Rule Definition dialog box appears.

④ Click the **Color** ☐ and select a color.

⑤ Click **OK**.

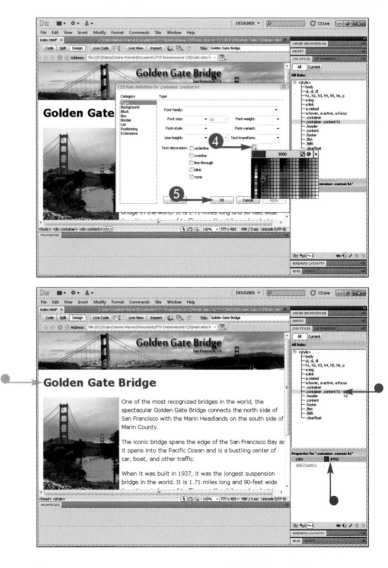

● The new style appears in the CSS Styles panel.

● The headline changes to the specified color.

● You can edit the style in the CSS Styles panel's Properties pane.

TIP

How do I change the font face and size of a headline?
In the steps shown here, you create a style when you change the color of the headline. By editing that same style, you can change the font face, font size, and other attributes. Just select the headline and then choose a font from the **Font** drop-down list in the Properties inspector.

Create a Compound Style

You can create styles using the class, tag, or ID selectors, or you can create a compound style that combines one or more styles to create a more specific style.

In the example shown in this section, a compound style is used to add a border to the image in the main area of the page without adding a border to the image in the header.

Create a Compound Style

Add a Border Only to a Main Image

*Note: If the CSS Styles panel is not open, click **Window** and then click **CSS Styles** to open it.*

1. Click to select the image in the main part of the page where you want to add a border.

2. Click ▣.

The New CSS Rule dialog box appears.

3. If it is not already selected, click ▼ and select **Compound**.

4. Make sure that the name is already entered into this field and that it ends with `img` for the image tag.

Note: In this example, the style `.container .content img` is created. This style will apply to an image only if it is contained within a style called `.content`, which is contained in a style called `.container`.

5. Click **OK**.

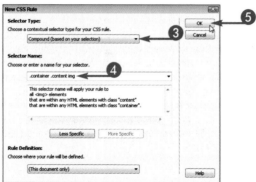

The CSS Rule Definition dialog box appears.

6 Click **Border**.

7 Click ▾ and select a border type.

8 Click ▾ and select a thickness.

9 Click ■ and select a color.

Note: In this example I added a solid, thin, black border.

10 Click **OK**.

● The new style appears in the CSS Styles panel and becomes available from the **Class** drop-down list in the Properties inspector.

● In this example, a border is added to the image in the main content area of the page.

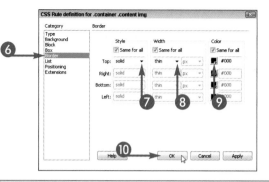

TIP

Why would I use a style to add a border instead of just using the Border field in the Properties inspector?

You can add, remove, or enlarge the border around an image by selecting the image and then entering a size in pixels in the **Border** field in the Properties inspector. If you set the border to **0**, it will not be visible. This is a common trick when you turn an image into a link and want to get rid of the blue border that indicates that the image is a link. Creating a style to control the border is a better option because you can add or remove a border from many images at once, and you can make changes to all the images later by changing one style, rather than having to change the border attribute for every image individually.

Create an AP Div with Content

AP Divs are scalable rectangles, inside of which you can place text, images, and just about anything else that you can include on a Web page. Although they work similarly to the divs used in Dreamweaver's CSS layouts, AP Divs include an Absolute Positioning setting, which means that they maintain their position on a page irrespective of the browser size.

Create an AP Div with Content

Create an AP Div

① Click ▾ and select **Layout** in the Insert panel.

② Click the **Draw AP Div** button (▣).

③ Click and drag to create an AP Div on the page.

You can resize and reposition an AP Div after you create it.

● The outline of the AP Div appears.

● You can click the tab in the upper-left corner of the AP Div to select it.

● When you select the AP Div, the Properties inspector displays the AP Div's properties.

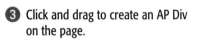

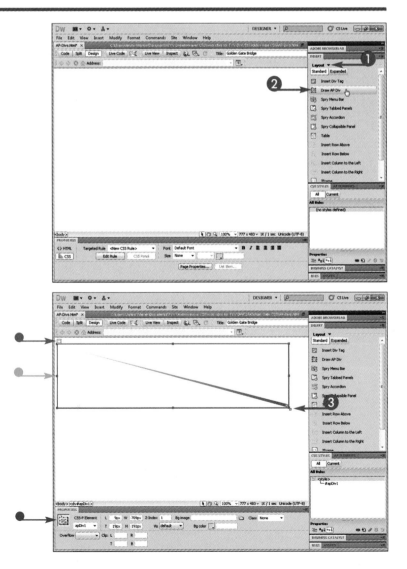

Add Content to an AP Div

① Click inside the AP Div.

② Click the element that you want to add in the Files panel and drag it into the AP Div.

● You can also insert an image by clicking **Insert** and then **Image** and selecting an image using the Insert Image dialog box.

You can add text by typing inside the AP Div.

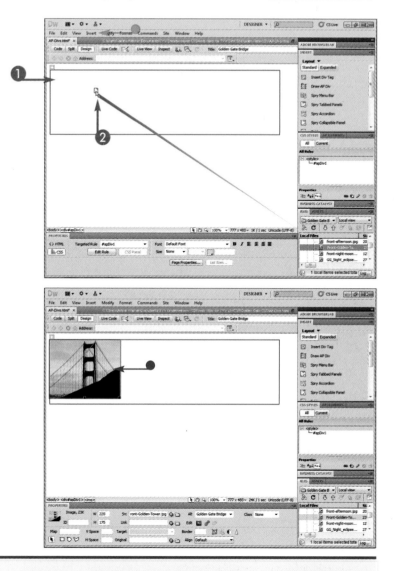

● The element is displayed inside the AP Div.

You can format text and images within an AP Div using the Properties inspector, just as you would format text or images anywhere else on a page.

Note: *To format text, see Chapter 5, "Formatting and Styling Text." For image options, see Chapter 6, "Working with Images and Multimedia."*

 TIPS

Should I use AP Divs to create a page layout?
Although AP Divs are very powerful layout tools, they are not the best option for creating an entire page layout. AP Divs serve as a nice complement to other page layout options, but when used exclusively, they create very inflexible designs that can look very different in different browsers.

What happens if a browser does not display AP Divs properly?
Although the latest versions of Internet Explorer and Firefox support AP Divs consistently, older browsers that do not support AP Divs may not display them as you intended. Similarly, text can get cut off if the font size is displayed larger than you intended in a browser and the text exceeds the size of the AP Div.

Resize and Reposition AP Divs

When you create a new AP Div, you can adjust its position and dimensions to make it fit attractively within the rest of the content on your page. One of the advantages of AP Divs is that you can move them easily by clicking and dragging them.

Resize and Reposition AP Divs

Click and Drag to Resize an AP Div

① Click the tab in the upper-left corner of the AP Div to select it.

● Square, blue handles appear around the edges of the AP Div.

② Click and drag one of the handles (↖ changes to ↘).

Dreamweaver resizes the AP Div to the new size.

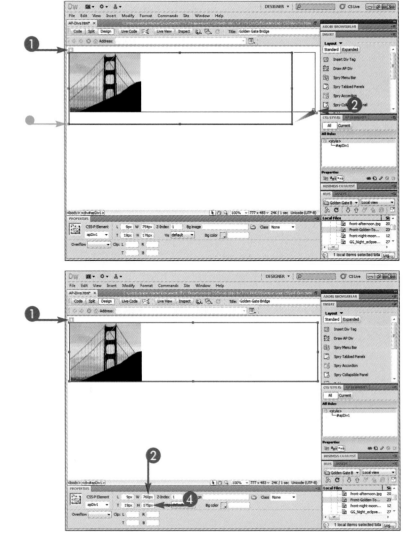

Resize with the Width and Height Attributes

① Click this tab.

② Type a new width in the **W** field.

③ Press Enter (Return).

Dreamweaver changes the AP Div's width.

④ Type a new height in the **H** field.

⑤ Press Enter (Return).

Dreamweaver changes the AP Div's height.

Reposition with the Cursor

1 Click and drag the tab in the upper-left corner of the AP Div to move it to a new position (⊹ changes to 🖑).

Dreamweaver moves the AP Div to the new location.

Reposition with the Left and Top Attributes

1 Click the AP Div's tab to select it.

2 Type the new distance from the left side of the window.

3 Press Enter (Return).

4 Type the new distance from the top of the window.

5 Press Enter (Return).

Dreamweaver applies the new positioning to the AP Div.

Note: *Setting left and top positioning to 0 puts the div in the top-left corner of a page.*

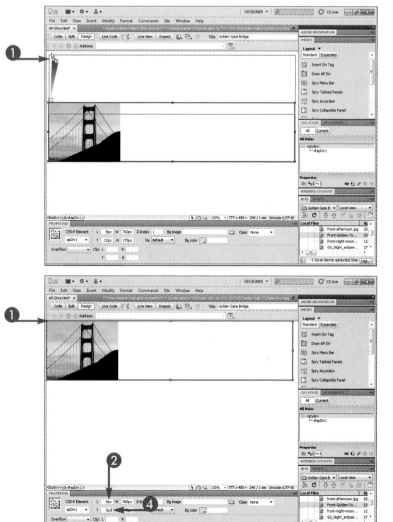

TIPS

How can I change the visibility of an AP Div?

To change an AP Div's visibility, select the AP Div and then click the **Vis** ▼ in the Properties inspector. You can make an AP Div visible or invisible. If it is a nested AP Div, it can inherit its characteristics from its parent, which is the enclosing AP Div.

Is there any other way to tell whether an AP Div is visible or invisible?

Yes. There is a visibility column available in the AP Elements tab in the CSS Styles panel. Click next to the AP Div name in the visibility column to adjust it. The open eye icon (👁) means that the AP Div is visible; the closed eye icon (👁) means that the AP Div is invisible. If no icon is showing, visibility is set to the default setting, and the AP Div appears visible or inherits its visibility.

Change the Stacking Order of AP Divs

You can change the stacking order of AP Divs on a page, thus affecting how they overlap one another. You can then hide parts of some AP Divs under other AP Divs.

Change the Stacking Order of AP Divs

Using the Z Index Attribute

Note: *If the CSS Styles panel is not open, click* **Window** *and then click* **CSS Styles** *to open it.*

1. Click the **AP Elements** tab.

2. Click the name of the AP Div whose order you want to change.

   When an AP Div is selected, it becomes visible in Dreamweaver's design area, even if it is covered by another AP Div.

3. Type a new number in the **Z** index field.

Note: *The higher the Z index of an AP Div, the higher it is placed in the stack.*

● Dreamweaver changes the stacking order of the AP Divs.

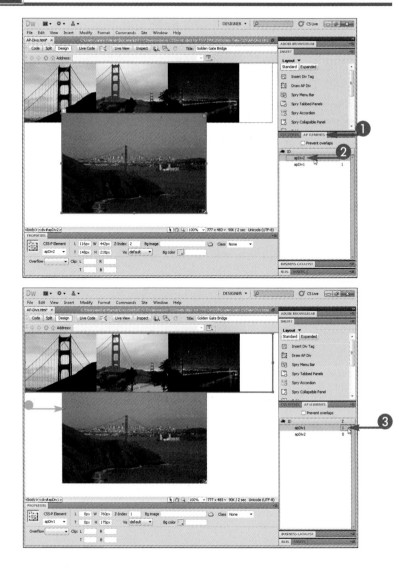

Reposition Stacked Divs

Note: If the CSS Styles panel is not open, click Window and then click CSS Styles to open it.

1. Click the **AP Elements** tab.

2. Click the tab of the AP Div that you want to select.

3. Click and drag the AP Div to reposition it on the page.

4. Change the stacking order number.

Note: You can change any or all of the AP div Z index numbers. Again, the higher the number, the higher the position.

Dreamweaver changes the stacking order of the AP Divs.

● If all or part of an AP Div is covered by another AP Div, it will not be visible on the page.

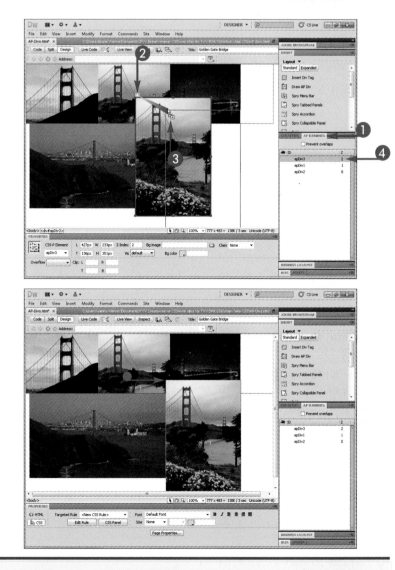

TIPS

Can I use any number for the Z index?

Yes. You can use any number for your Z index. If you are working with many AP Divs on a page, a good technique is to number them as 10, 20, 30, and so on, instead of 1, 2, and 3. That way, if you want to position an AP Div between existing AP Divs, you can number it something like 15 or 25, and you do not have to renumber all the other AP Divs to accommodate its new position.

How do I change the name of an AP Div?

You can change the name of an AP Div in the Properties inspector. First, select the AP Div by clicking its name in the AP Elements panel or by clicking to select the AP Div in the design area of the page. In the **Name** field, in the top-left corner of the Properties inspector, you see the current name displayed as text. Simply select the text and type the new name.

Create a Nested AP Div

A nested AP Div is often called a *child AP Div*, and the AP Div that contains the nested AP Div is called the *parent*. They act as a unit on the page; if the parent AP Div moves, the child goes with it. Similarly, the positioning of the child is based on the position of the parent.

You can move the child AP Div independently of the parent, but the AP Divs always stay linked unless you drag the nested AP Div out from under the parent.

Create a Nested AP Div

*Note: If the AP Elements panel is not open, click **Window** and then click **CSS Styles**. Then click the **AP Elements** tab.*

1 Click .

2 Click and drag to create an AP Div.

Dreamweaver inserts an AP Div into the page.

You can insert text, images, or tables into the AP Div.

● In this example, text is placed in the first AP Div.

3 Click .

4 Click and drag to create a second AP Div inside the first AP Div.

● The name of the second AP Div appears in the AP Elements panel.

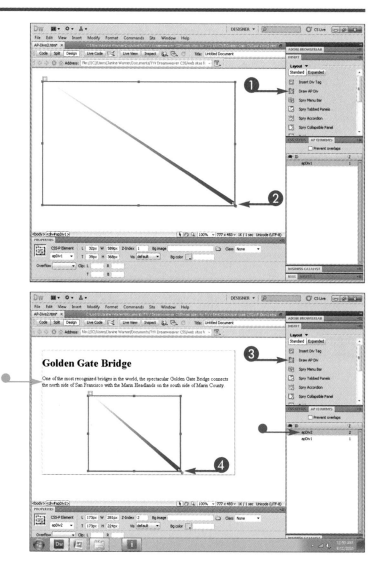

● You can insert text, images, or tables into the second AP Div.

Note: *In this example, an image is placed in the second AP Div.*

5 Click and drag to move the first AP Div on the page.

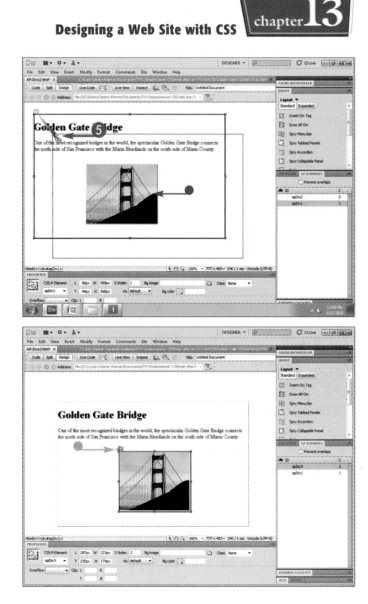

● If the nested, *or child,* AP Div does not move with the parent AP Div, click the tab and drag to reposition it.

TIP

Can I free a nested AP Div?

Yes, you can take a nested AP Div out of its parent AP Div. To do so, click **Window**, then click **CSS Styles**, and then click the **AP Elements** tab to open the AP Divs panel. Click the nested AP Div and drag it above the parent AP Div. The AP Div appears on its own line in the AP Elements panel, and the layer is no longer nested. This does not change the location of the AP Div on the page, but it allows you to move the AP Div independently of its parent.

CHAPTER

14

Publishing a Web Site

After you are done building your Web pages, you can publish your site on a server where anyone with an Internet connection can view them. This chapter shows you how to publish your Web site and keep it up to date with Dreamweaver.

Publish Your Web Site

Most designers build and test their Web sites on their local computers and then transfer them to a Web server when they are ready to publish them on the Internet. A *Web server* is an Internet-connected computer running special software that enables the computer to serve files to Web browsers. Dreamweaver includes tools that enable you to connect and transfer pages to a Web server.

Publish Your Web Site

To publish your site files using Dreamweaver, follow these steps:

1. Identify the main folder on your computer where all your Web site files are kept.

Note: *To define a local site, see Chapter 2, "Setting Up Your Web Site."*

2. Enter the Web server information to publish your files.

Note: *To define a remote site, see the section "Set Up a Remote Site."*

Most people publish their Web pages on servers maintained by their Internet service provider (ISP), a Web-hosting company, or their company or school.

3. Connect to the Web server and transfer the files.

The Site window displays a user-friendly interface for organizing your files and transferring them to the remote site.

After uploading your site, you can update it by editing the copies of the site files on your computer (the local site) and then transferring those copies to the Web server (the remote site).

With the Site window, you can view the organization of all the files in your site. You can also upload local files to the remote site and download remote files to the local site through the Files panel. You can access the Site window by clicking the Expand/Collapse button in the Files panel. For more information about the Files panel, see Chapter 3, "Exploring the Dreamweaver Interface."

Local files

The right pane displays all the files in the root folder of your local computer.

Remote site

The left pane displays all the files in your site that have been published to the remote Web server.

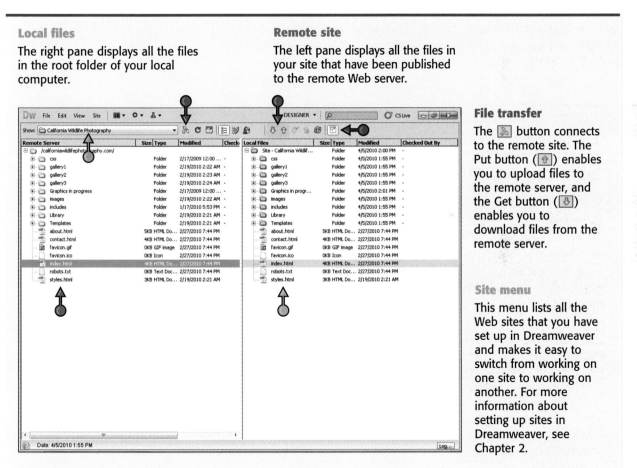

File transfer

The 🔌 button connects to the remote site. The Put button (⬆) enables you to upload files to the remote server, and the Get button (⬇) enables you to download files from the remote server.

Site menu

This menu lists all the Web sites that you have set up in Dreamweaver and makes it easy to switch from working on one site to working on another. For more information about setting up sites in Dreamweaver, see Chapter 2.

Expand/Collapse Files panel

You can click the Expand/Collapse button (🗗) to expand the Files panel to two panes. With the Files panel expanded, you can see the local and remote sites simultaneously, making it easier to upload and download files. To close the expanded view and return the Files panel to one column, click 🗗 again.

Add Web Browsers for Testing Pages

Because Web pages do not always look the same in different Web browsers, it is important to test your pages in more than one browser to make sure that they will look good to everyone who visits your site. Dreamweaver makes it easy to add browsers to the Preview menu, and I recommend that you test your site in the latest version of Internet Explorer and Firefox. It is also a good practice to test your pages in Safari, which is popular on Macintosh computers, and Google Chrome, the newest browser on the Web, which is quickly growing in popularity.

Add Web Browsers for Testing Pages

1. Click **File**.
2. Click **Preview in Browser**.
3. Click **Edit Browser List**.

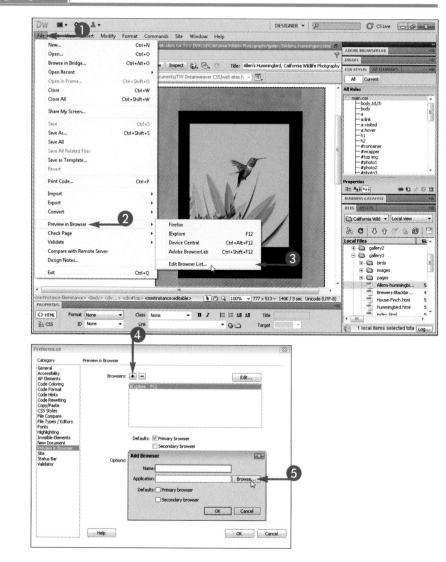

The Preferences dialog box appears.

4. Click in the Preview in Browser area.

The Add Browser dialog box appears.

5. Click **Browse**.

The Select Browser dialog box appears.

6 Click ▼ and select the folder that contains the browser application.

7 Click the browser application that you want to add.

8 Click **Open**.

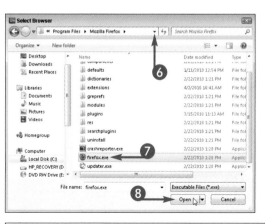

You are returned to the Add Browser dialog box.

9 Click **OK**.

You are returned to the Preferences dialog box.

10 Repeat steps **4** to **9** to add additional browsers.

11 Click **OK**.

The browsers are added to the Preview in Browser list.

TIPS

Why do Web pages not look the same in different browsers?

In the early days of the Web, sites had only simple HTML and images. With more advanced options, such as CSS and multimedia, Web browsers evolved. Unfortunately, many people still have older browsers that do not support all the latest design options, and not all browser makers updated their programs in the same ways.

What is the most popular browser?

There are dozens of browsers in use on the Web, but the most popular are Microsoft Internet Explorer, Mozilla Firefox, Apple Safari, Google Chrome, and Opera. There are also special browsers, called *screen readers,* that read Web pages to users.

Preview Your Pages in Multiple Web Browsers

Before you publish your Web site, it is always a good practice to test your pages on your local computer first. You can preview an HTML page in any browser that is installed on your computer and set it up for preview, as described in the preceding section, "Add Web Browsers for Testing Pages."

Preview Your Pages in Multiple Web Browsers

1 Click **File**.

2 Click **Preview in Browser**.

3 Click any of the Web browsers.

You can also preview the page in the browser you have designated as primary by pressing F12.

The Web browser launches and displays the page.

Note: When you preview a Web page on your computer in a browser, you can follow links and use other interactive features, just as you would when viewing a Web page in a browser on the Internet.

④ In Dreamweaver, click **File**.

⑤ Click **Preview in Browser**.

⑥ Click a different Web browser.

The Web browser launches and displays the page.

Note: It is a good practice to test your pages in as many Web browsers as possible.

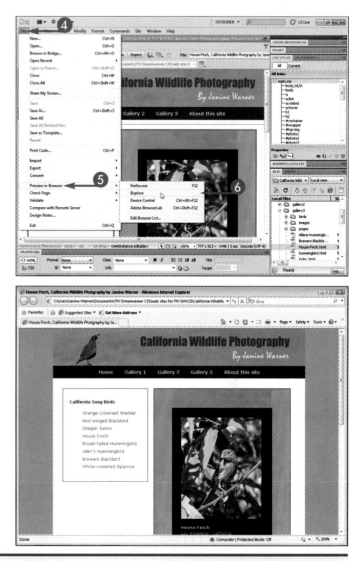

TIP

What if I do not have all the Web browsers I should use to test my Web pages?

In addition to testing your pages with multiple Web browsers on your own computer, you can test your pages after they are published on a Web server by using one of the many Web browser tools that simulate the way different Web browsers work. These tools are especially useful for testing your pages in older Web browsers, which are harder to find for use on your own computer. Some of the most popular online Web browser testing tools are the Browser Sandbox, at http://spoon.net/browsers/, Browsershots, at www.browsershots.org/, and CrossBrowserTesting, at www.crossbrowsertesting.com/.

Organize Your Files and Folders

You can use the Files panel to organize the files and folders that make up your Web site. With this panel, you can create and delete files and folders, as well as move files between folders; Dreamweaver automatically fixes any associated links and inserted images.

Creating subfolders to organize files of a similar type can be useful if you have a large Web site.

① Click **Window**.

② Click **Files**.

The Files panel is displayed.

③ Click ▼ to display the contents of the site.

④ Click + to view the files in a subfolder (+ changes to –).

The folder contents are displayed.

● You can click – to close the subfolder.

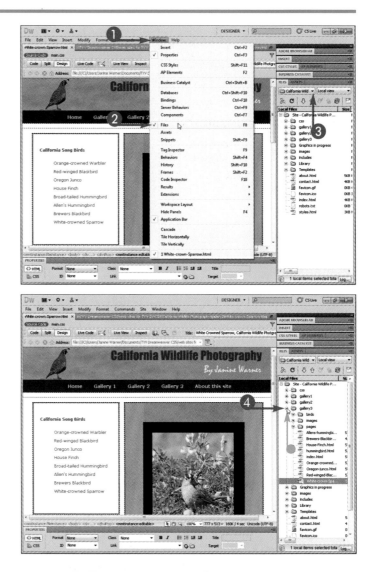

⑤ To move a file in your local site folder into a subfolder, click and drag it to the new subfolder (⟨↖⟩ changes to ⟨↙⟩).

● To move multiple files at once, hold down the **Shift** key and click to select a group of files simultaneously.

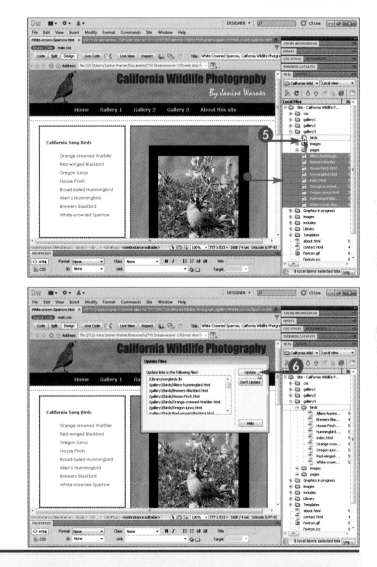

The Update Files dialog box appears, asking if you want to update your links.

⑥ Click **Update** to keep your local site links from breaking.

Dreamweaver automatically makes any changes necessary to preserve the links.

TIPS

What happens to links when I move files?

When you create a hyperlink from one page to another, Dreamweaver creates the necessary name and location link HTML code. If you move or rename files after they are used in a link, the link code must be updated, or the link will be broken. When you use the Files panel to move or rename files or to move files into subfolders, Dreamweaver keeps track of any affected code and updates it automatically.

Should I use subfolders?

Organizing your text, image, and multimedia files in subfolders can help you keep track of the contents of your Web site. Although you can store all the files on your site in one main folder, most designers find it easier to find files when the files are organized in subfolders, such as an Images folder for photos and other graphics.

Set Up a Remote Site

Before you can publish your Web site in Dreamweaver, you need to set up the remote site to create a connection to your Web server. You set up a remote site by entering the FTP information, including your username and password, for your Web server. You can then use Dreamweaver to transfer your files from your computer to the remote server.

Note: **Before you can set up a remote site, you need to set up your local site and define it in Dreamweaver. To do so, see Chapter 2.**

Set Up a Remote Site

1. Click **Site**.

2. Click **Manage Sites**.

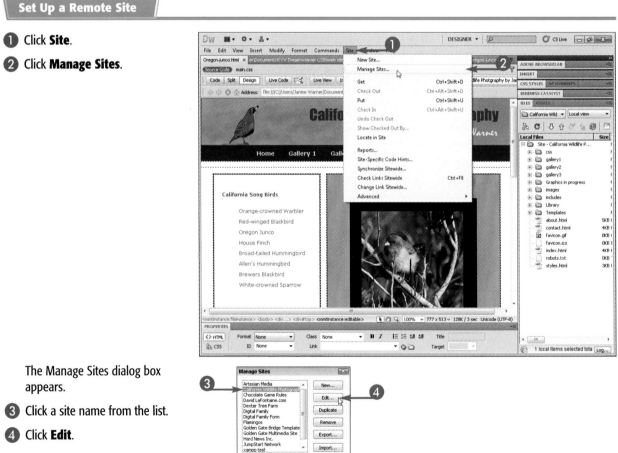

The Manage Sites dialog box appears.

3. Click a site name from the list.

4. Click **Edit**.

The Site Setup dialog box appears.

5 Click **Servers**.

6 Click ⊞.

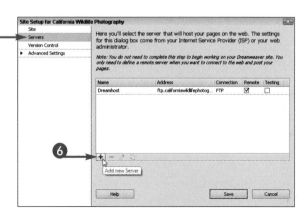

A dialog box appears.

7 Type a name to identify the server setup.

8 Click ▾ and select **FTP**.

Note: FTP is the most common way to transfer a Web site to a Web server.

9 Type the name of the FTP host (Web server).

10 Type your login name and password.

11 Type the directory path of your site on the Web server.

● You can click **Test** to confirm the Web server information.

12 Click **Save**.

13 Click **Save**.

14 Click **Done** in the Manage Sites dialog box.

The remote site is now set up.

What happens if I change my ISP, and I need to move my site to a different server?

You need to change your remote site settings to enable Dreamweaver to connect to your new Web server. Your local site settings can stay the same. Make sure that you keep your local files current and backed up before you change servers.

How do I register a domain name?

You can register a domain name at a number of domain registration services on the Internet. Two of the most popular, and least expensive, are www.godaddy.com and www.1and1.com. As long as you pay the annual fee, which is less than $10 a year at these sites, the domain is yours. To direct the domain to your Web site, you need to specify where your Web server is at the domain registration service.

Connect to a Remote Site

You can connect to the Web server that hosts your remote site and transfer files between it and Dreamweaver. Dreamweaver connects to the Web server by a process known as *file transfer protocol*, or *FTP*.

Before you can connect to a remote server, you need to set up your remote site. For more information, see the preceding section, "Set Up a Remote Site."

Connect to a Remote Site

① In the Files panel, click the Expand button (🗐) to expand the remote and local site panels.

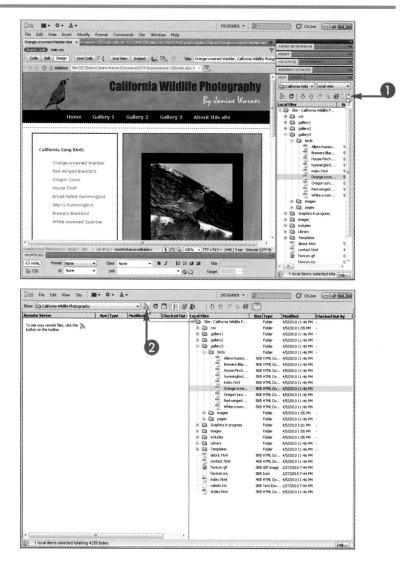

The Files panel expands to fill the screen.

② Click the Connect button (🔌) to connect to the Web server.

Note: *Dreamweaver displays an alert dialog box if it cannot connect to the site. If you have trouble connecting, review the host information that you entered for the remote site.*

● When you are connected to the Internet, 🔲 changes to 🔲.

Dreamweaver displays the contents of the remote site's host directory.

③ Click + to view the contents of a directory on the Web server (+ changes to –).

Dreamweaver displays the contents of the directory.

④ Click 🔲 to disconnect.

Dreamweaver disconnects from the Web server.

If you do not transfer any files for 30 minutes, Dreamweaver automatically disconnects from the Web server.

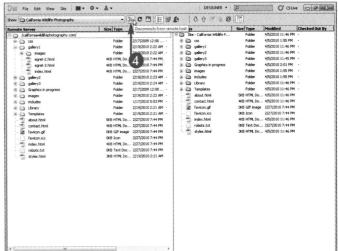

 TIPS

How do I keep Dreamweaver from prematurely disconnecting from the Web server?

You can click **Edit** ➪ **Preferences** ➪ **Site**. You can change the time that Dreamweaver allows to pass between commands before it logs you off the server — the default is 30 minutes. Note that Web servers also have a similar setting on their end. Therefore, the server, not Dreamweaver, may sometimes log you off if you are inactive for more than the server's allotted time.

What if the connection does not work?

If Dreamweaver fails to connect to your server, your Internet connection may be down. Make sure that your computer is connected to the Internet and try again. If you still cannot connect, you may have incorrectly entered the FTP settings. Check with your service provider or system administrator if you are not sure about your Web server settings.

Upload Files to a Web Server

You can use Dreamweaver's FTP features to upload files from your local site to your remote server to make your Web pages available to others on the Internet.

Upload Files to a Web Server

Publish Files Online

1. Click 🖳 to connect to the Web server through the Site window (🖳 changes to 🖳).

2. Click the file that you want to upload.

3. Click the Put button (⬆).

● You can also right-click the file and select **Put** from the menu that appears.

A dialog box appears, asking if you want to include dependent files.

Note: Dependent files are images and other files associated with a particular page.

4. Click **Yes** or **No**.

Note: If you do nothing, after 30 seconds, the file and related files will be transferred automatically.

● You can click here (□ changes to ☑) to avoid seeing this dialog box again.

● The file transfers from your computer to the Web, and the filename appears in the Remote files panel.

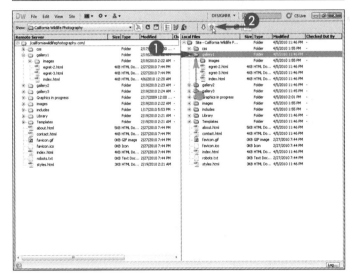

Upload a Folder

1. In the right pane, right-click the folder that you want to upload.

2. Click .

● You can also right-click the folder and select **Put** from the menu that appears.

Dreamweaver transfers the folder and its contents from your computer to the Web server.

TIPS

How do I stop a file transfer in progress?

You can click **Cancel** in the Status dialog box that appears when a transfer is in progress. You can also press Esc to cancel a file transfer.

How can I delete a file from the Web server?

With the Site window open, connect to the Web server. When the list of files appears in the left pane, click the file that you want to delete and then press Del. A dialog box appears, asking if you really want to delete the selected file. Click **OK**. You can also delete multiple files and folders.

Download Files from a Web Server

You can download files from your Web server in Dreamweaver if you need to retrieve them. After they are downloaded, you can make changes or updates to the pages in Dreamweaver and then put them back on the Web server.

Download Files from a Web Server

Download Files

1 Click 🔲 to connect to the Web server (🔲 changes to 🔲).

2 Click the file that you want to download.

3 Click the Get button (🔲).

● You can also right-click the file on the remote site and select **Get** from the menu that appears.

A dialog box appears, asking if you want to include dependent files.

Note: Dependent files are images and other files associated with a particular page.

4 Click **Yes** or **No**.

● You can click the check box (🔲 changes to 🔲) to avoid seeing this dialog box again.

● The Background File Activity dialog box appears when Dreamweaver needs to reestablish a connection to the server to complete the upload or download process.

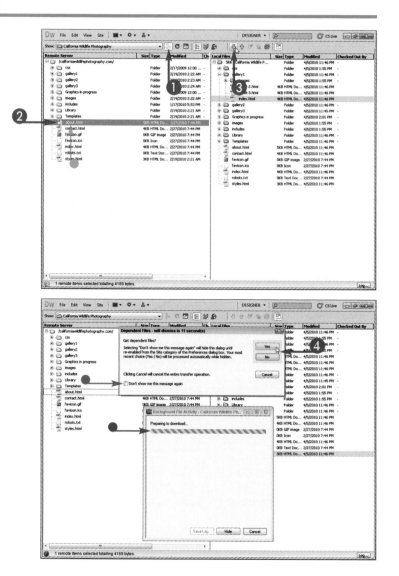

● The file transfers from the Web server to your computer.

If the file already exists on your local computer, a dialog box appears, asking whether it is okay to overwrite it.

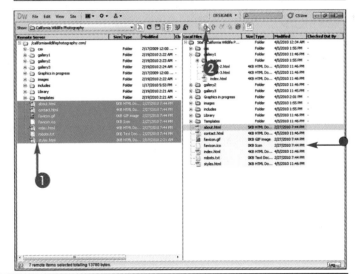

Download Multiple Files

①	Press and hold **Ctrl** (**Control**) and click to select the files that you want to download.

②	Click 🔽.

The files transfer from your Web server to your computer.

● The downloaded files appear in the Local Files panel.

TIPS

Where does Dreamweaver log errors that occur during file transfer?

Dreamweaver logs all transfer activity, including errors, in a file-transfer log. You can view it by clicking **Window**, then clicking **Results**, and then clicking **FTP Log**. The FTP Log panel appears at the bottom of the screen.

Can I use my Web site to store files while I am still working on them?

If a file is on your Web server, it can be viewed on the Internet. When pages are under construction and you do not want them to be seen, you should not put them up on your Web site, even temporarily. Even if the page is not linked to your site, someone may find it, or a search engine may even index and cache it.

Synchronize Your Local and Remote Sites

Dreamweaver can synchronize files between your local and remote sites so that both sites have an identical set of the most recent files. This can be useful if other people are editing the files on the remote site and you need to update your local copies of those files. It is also handy if you edit pages and you do not remember all the pages that you need to upload.

① Click 📷 to connect to the Web server (📷 changes to 📷).

② Click the Synchronize button (📷).

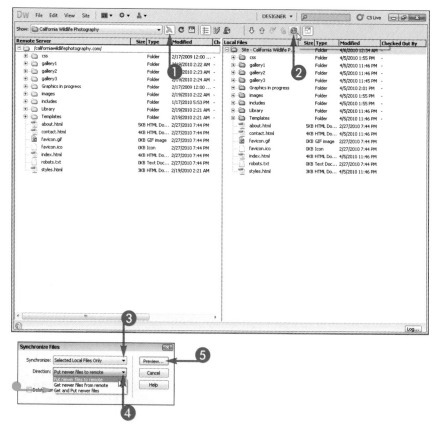

The Synchronize Files dialog box appears.

③ Click ▼ and select the files that you want to synchronize.

④ Click ▼ and select the direction that you want to copy the files.

● You can place the newest copies on both the remote and local sites by selecting **Get and Put newer files**.

⑤ Click **Preview**.

Dreamweaver compares the sites and then lists the files for transfer, based on your selections in steps **3** and **4**.

6 Click the files that you do not want to transfer.

7 With the files selected, click the Trash button (🗑) to remove them from the transfer list.

8 Click **OK**.

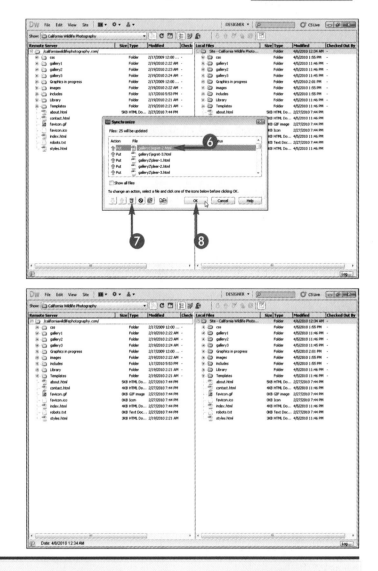

Dreamweaver transfers the files.

The local and remote sites are now synchronized.

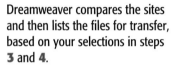

Are there other FTP tools besides those available from Dreamweaver?

Dreamweaver offers the convenience of transferring files without having to open other programs. However, the application uses many system resources and can significantly slow down some computers. There are many good alternatives available. For example, in Windows, you can use WS_FTP. On Mac OS, you can use Transmit or Fetch. You can download evaluation copies of these programs from www.download.com. Other alternatives for transferring files through FTP include CuteFTP, LeechFTP, and CoffeeCup Direct FTP.

Maintaining a Web Site

Maintaining a Web site and keeping its content fresh can be as much work as creating the site. Dreamweaver's site-maintenance tools make updating faster and easier.

Dreamweaver's visual aids make is possible to see things that are not there, such as the outline of a `div` tag or the border of a table. These visual aids make it easier to manage the features of your site and to edit your page designs.

Although visual aids are helpful, sometimes you may prefer to turn them off so that you can see how your designs will look without all the borders and outlines.

View Visual Aids

1 Click the Visual Aids button ().

2 Click **CSS Layout Outlines**.

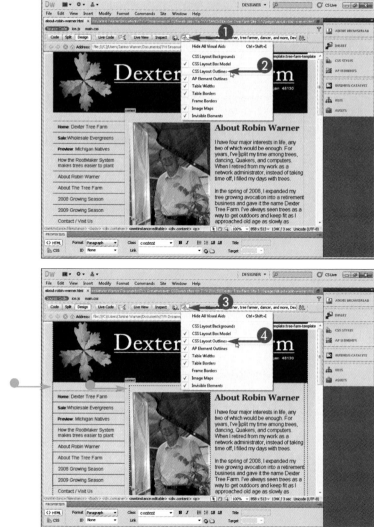

● A dotted line appears around any `div` tags or other CSS layout elements.

3 Click again.

4 Click **CSS Layout Outlines** again to remove ✓.

The dotted lines around CSS layout elements disappear.

⑤ Click 🔲 again.

⑥ Click **Hide All Visual Aids**.

All visual aids disappear.

Are visual aids displayed in a Web browser?

No. Visual aids are visible only in the Dreamweaver workspace. Visual aids are designed to provide additional information and guides as you work on a page layout, but they will not be visible when your visitors to your site view your page designs in a Web browser.

Is there a shortcut to hide all visual aids?

Yes. Like many features in Dreamweaver, you can use a keyboard shortcut instead of selecting an option from a menu or panel. To hide all visual aids at once, press **Ctrl** plus **Shift** plus the letter *I* (on a Windows computer). If you are using a Mac, press ⌘ plus **Shift** plus the letter *I*. To turn visual aids back on, press the same keys in combination again.

Manage Site Assets

You can view and manage elements that appear in the pages of your site with the Assets panel. The Assets panel provides an easy way to insert elements that you want to use more than once in your site.

1 Click **Window**.

2 Click **Assets**.

● You can also click the **Assets** tab in the Files panel to open the Assets panel.

The Assets panel appears, displaying objects from the selected category.

3 Click an icon to display its collection of assets.

Note: *In this example, the image assets are shown.*

4 Click the name of any asset to preview it in the Assets panel.

● You can click and drag the side of the Assets panel to expand it.

The Assets panel is displayed in the new dimensions and previews your selected asset.

⑤ Click a column heading.

The assets are now sorted by the selected column heading in ascending order.

If you click the name of the column that the assets are already sorted by, the asset order switches to descending order.

● To view other assets, you can click a different category button.

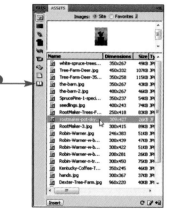

TIP

How are assets organized?
Items in the Assets panel are organized into the following categories:

	Images	GIF, JPG, and PNG images
	Color	Text, background, link, and style-sheet colors
	URLs	Accessible external Web addresses
	Flash	Flash-based multimedia
	Shockwave	Shockwave-based multimedia
	Movie	QuickTime and MPEG movies
	Scripts	External JavaScript or VBScript files
	Templates	Page-layout templates
	Library	Library of reusable page elements

Add Content with the Assets Panel

You can add frequently used content to your site directly from the Assets panel. This technique can be more efficient than using a menu command or the Insert panel.

① Click the **Assets** tab to open the Assets panel.

② Click a category.

③ Click the asset that you want to add.

④ Drag the asset onto the page.

If the asset is an image, the Image Tag Accessibility Attributes dialog box appears.

⑤ Type a description of the image.

● Entering a long description URL is optional.

⑥ Click **OK**.

Dreamweaver inserts the asset into your Document window.

Note: *In this example, an image is added to the page.*

⑦ Click to select the image or other asset.

⑧ Edit the asset as you would any other asset.

Note: *In this example, an image alignment option is applied.*

Dreamweaver applies your changes to the asset in the Document window.

● In this example, the image is aligned to the right.

How do I copy assets from one site to another?

Click one or more items in the Assets panel and then right-click (Control + click) the selected assets. From the menu that appears, click **Copy to Site** and then click a site to which you want to copy the assets. The assets appear in the Favorites list under the same category in the other site.

Are all my links saved in the Assets panel?

Only links to external Web sites and email addresses are saved in the Assets panel. Links to internal pages in your site are not saved in the Assets panel. You can use the saved links in the Assets panel to quickly create new links to Web sites and email addresses to which you have already linked in your site.

Specify Favorite Assets

To make your asset lists more manageable, you can organize assets that you use often into a Favorites list inside each asset category.

Add an Asset to the Favorites List

① Click the **Assets** tab to open the Assets panel.

② Click the category containing the asset that you want to add to the Favorites list.

③ Click the asset.

④ Right-click (`Control` + click) the selected asset and click **Add to Favorites** on the menu that appears.

Dreamweaver adds the asset to the category's Favorites list.

⑤ Click **Favorites** (◎ changes to ◉).

● The selected asset appears in the Favorites category.

Nickname a Favorite Asset

① Click the category containing the favorite that you want to nickname.

② Click **Favorites** (◎ changes to ◉).

Note: You cannot nickname regular assets — only assets that have been added to the Favorites list.

③ Right-click (Control + click) the asset.

④ Click **Edit Nickname**.

⑤ Type a nickname.

⑥ Press Enter (Return).

The nickname appears in the Favorites list.

 TIPS

How do I remove an item entirely from the Assets panel?

To delete an asset, you need to delete the corresponding file from the Files panel. Click **Window** and then click **Files** or click the Files tab to open the Files panel. Click the name of the file and then press Del or Backspace.

How do I add items to the Assets panel?

You do not need to add items. One of the handiest things about the Assets panel is that every time you add an image, external link, email link, color, or multimedia asset to your Web site, Dreamweaver automatically stores it in the Assets panel.

Check a Page In or Out

Dreamweaver provides a Check In/Check Out system that keeps track of files when a team is working on a Web site. When one person checks out a page from the Web server, others cannot access the same file.

The Check In/Check Out feature can slow down some Dreamweaver operations and is not recommended if you are not working with others on the same site.

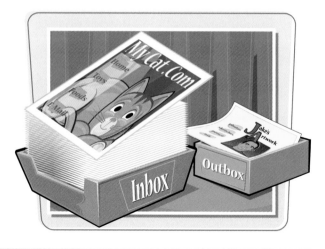

Check a Page In or Out

Enable Check In/Check Out

Note: You first need to specify the remote settings and connect to your remote Web server to use the Check In/Check Out function. To set up a remote site and connect to it, see Chapter 14, "Publishing a Web Site."

1 Click **Site**.

2 Click **Manage Sites**.

The Manage Sites dialog box appears.

3 Click the site name.

4 Click **Edit**.

The Site Setup dialog box appears.

5 Click **Servers**.

6 Click the name of the server to select it.

Note: This is the server you set up in Chapter 14.

7 Click .

A dialog box appears.

⑧ Click the **Advanced** tab.

⑨ Click **Enable file check-out**
(☐ changes to ☑).

⑩ Type your name and email address.

⑪ Click **Save**.

⑫ Click **Save** in the Site Setup dialog box.

⑬ Click **Done** in the Manage Sites
dialog box.

Check In/Check Out is now enabled.

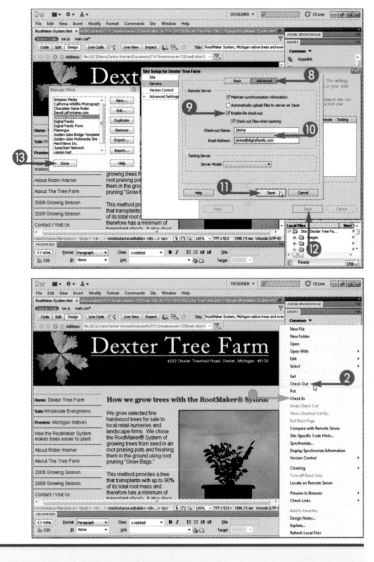

Check Out a File

① Click the file in the Files panel if it
is not checked out and then right-
click (Control + click) it.

② Click **Check Out**.

Dreamweaver marks the page as
checked out.

● To check in a file, repeat step **1**
and click **Check In** in step **2**.

TIPS

How is a file marked as checked out?

When you check out a file,
Dreamweaver creates a temporary
LCK file that is stored in the
remote site folder while the page
is checked out. The file contains
information about who has
checked the file out. Dreamweaver
does not display the LCK files in the file list, but
you can see them if you access your remote site
with a different FTP program.

Can I email someone who has a file checked out to tell them that I need it?

Yes. Dreamweaver collects
usernames and email
addresses in the Check In and
Check Out fields to make it
easy for multiple people who
are working on the same Web site to stay in touch.
If someone else has a file checked out, you can
use the Check In/Check Out feature to send them
an email message.

Make Design Notes

If you are working on a site collaboratively, design notes enable you to add information about the development status of a file. For example, you can attach information to your Web pages, such as a request to have a page edited before it is published.

1. Open the Web page to which you want to attach a design note.

2. Click **File**.

3. Click **Design Notes**.

The Design Notes dialog box appears.

4. Click ![] and select a status for the page.

5. Type a note.

6. Click the Date button (![]) to enter the current date in the Notes field.

● You can click **Show when file is opened** (![] changes to ![]) to automatically show design notes when a file opens.

7. Click the **All info** tab.

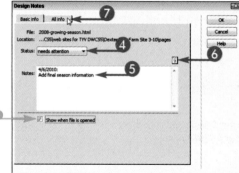

The All info tab is displayed.

⑧ To enter new information in the Design Notes dialog box, click ⊞.

⑨ Type a name and associated value.

● The added value pair appears in the Info section.

● You can delete information by clicking it in the Info section and then clicking ⊟.

⑩ Click **OK**.

Dreamweaver attaches the design note to the page.

How can I view design notes?

You can view design notes in two ways: First, files with a design note have a yellow bubble in the Sites window. Double-click it to open the design note. Alternatively, you can open any file with an attached design note, then click **File**, and then click **Design Notes** to open the design note.

Are design notes private?

Although design notes are not linked to the page or displayed in a Web browser, anyone with access to your server can view your design notes. If someone is especially clever and your server does not protect the notes folder, then he or she may find it, even without password access to your site. Ultimately, design notes are useful for communication among Web designers, but they are not meant to protect important secrets.

Run a Site Report

Running a site report can help you pinpoint problems in your site, including redundant HTML code in your pages and missing page titles. It is a good idea to test your site by running a report before you upload it to a Web server.

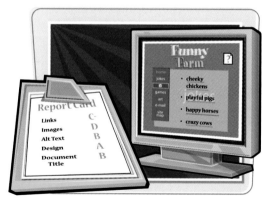

① Click **Site**.

② Click **Reports**.

The Reports dialog box appears.

③ Click ▼ and select to run a report on either the entire site or selected files.

④ Click the reports that you want to run (☐ changes to ☑).

⑤ Click **Run**.

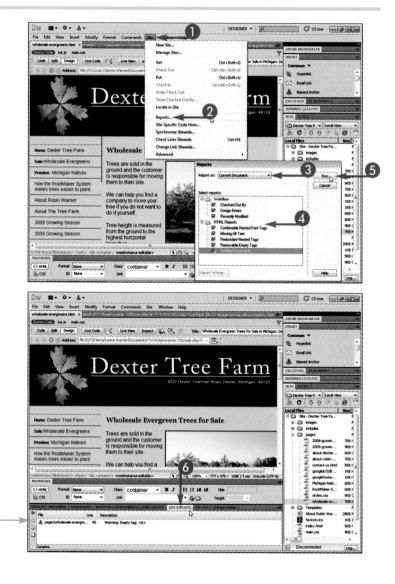

● Dreamweaver creates a report and displays it in the Results panel of the Properties inspector.

⑥ Click any tab across the top of the Results panel to display that report.

286

Change a Link Sitewide

You can search and replace all the hyperlinks on your site that point to a specific address. This is helpful when a page is renamed or deleted and the links to it need to be updated.

① Click **Site**.

② Click **Change Link Sitewide**.

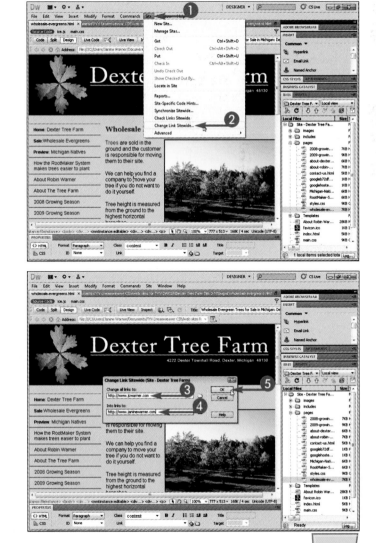

The Change Link Sitewide dialog box appears.

③ Type the old hyperlink destination that you want to change.

④ Type the new hyperlink destination.

Note: Email links must begin with mailto: and include the full email address. You must enter the full URL to change links to another Web site.

⑤ Click **OK**.

Dreamweaver finds and replaces all instances of the link. A dialog box asks you to confirm the changes.

Find and Replace Text

The Find and Replace feature is a powerful tool for making changes to text elements that repeat across many pages. You can find and replace text on your Web page, your source code, or specific HTML tags in your pages.

① Click **Edit**.

② Click **Find and Replace**.

The Find and Replace dialog box appears.

③ Click ▾ and select whether you want to search the entire site or only selected files.

④ Click ▾ and select the type of text that you want to search.

● For example, you can select **Text (Advanced)** to find text that is inside a specific tag.

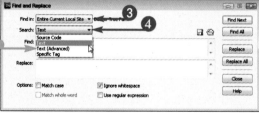

⑤ Type the text that you want to find.

● You can click **Find Next** to find instances of your query one at a time.

⑥ Type the replacement text.

⑦ Click **Replace** to replace the text instances one at a time.

● You can also click **Replace All** to automatically replace all instances of your text search.

If you are using search and replace for the entire site, Dreamweaver asks whether you want to replace text in unopened documents; click **Yes**.

● Dreamweaver replaces the text, and the details appear in the bottom of the screen in the Reports panel.

TIPS

Can I use the Find and Replace feature to alter HTML code?

Yes. Searching for a string of code is a quick way to make changes to a Web site. For example, if you want to alter the body color for every page, you can search for the HTML `<body>` tag and replace it with a different color tag.

Can I use the Find and Replace feature to alter an HTML attribute?

Yes. You can replace attributes to achieve many things. For example, you can change the color of specific text in your page (change `color="green"` to `color="red"` in `<font>` tags) or change the page background color across your site (change `bgcolor="black"` to `bgcolor="white"` in `<body>` tags).

16

Adding Interactivity with Spry and JavaScript

When you are ready to move onto some of the more advanced features in Dreamweaver, this chapter is for you. Using Dreamweaver's behaviors, you can create JavaScript features, such as rollover effects. Using the Spry widgets, you can create more advanced interactive features, such as drop-down menus.

Introducing Spry and Behaviors

Some of the most advanced Web site features are created by combining HTML and CSS with more advanced technologies, such as JavaScript. To help you create these features without having to write the code yourself, Dreamweaver includes a collection of widgets and behaviors that you can use on your Web pages. You will find these features under the Spry menu and in the Behaviors panel.

Behavior Basics

Behaviors are cause-and-effect events that you can insert into your Web pages. For example, you can use the Rollover Image behavior to add an image to a page and then replace that image with another image when a visitor rolls a cursor over the first image. Similarly, the Open Browser Window behavior causes a new Web browser window to open when a user clicks or moves the cursor over an image.

Behaviors and Browsers

Because behaviors vary in complexity, they are written in various ways to ensure compatibility with older Web browsers. The latest versions of both Internet Explorer and Firefox display most of Dreamweaver's behaviors well, and you can disable behaviors that may not work in older Web browsers.

Behind the Scenes

Dreamweaver creates most behaviors with *JavaScript* and creates Spry features, such as drop-down menus, by combining JavaScript and XML. CSS is also a key component of many of these advanced features. Even if you are familiar with HTML code, you may be surprised by how complex JavaScript looks when you view the code behind your pages.

Create a Drop-Down Menu

You can create many interactive features using Dreamweaver's Spry widgets. One of the most popular is a drop-down menu, which makes it possible to include a drop-down list of links in a navigation bar.

Create a Drop-Down Menu

Note: If the Insert panel is not open, click **Window** and then click **Insert** to open it.

1. Click to place your cursor where you want to add the menu.

2. Click ▾.

3. Click **Spry**.

The Spry Insert panel appears.

4. Click **Spry Menu Bar**.

The Spry Menu Bar dialog box appears.

5. Click **Horizontal** (◎ changes to ◉).

6. Click **OK**.

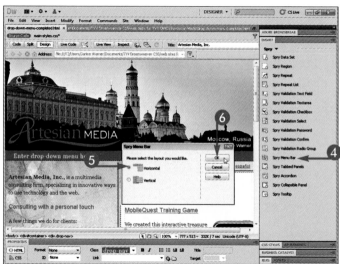

A Spry menu bar appears in the workspace.

⑦ Click the blue Spry menu bar.

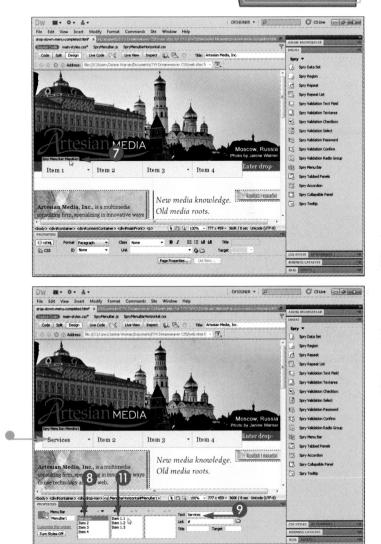

The menu bar properties appear in the Properties inspector.

⑧ Click **Item 1**.

⑨ Type a name for the menu item in the **Text** field.

⑩ Press Enter (Return).

● The name appears in the workspace and in the Properties inspector.

⑪ Click **Item 1.1**.

What are Spry widgets?

Spry widgets are a set of features designed to make it easy to add a variety of complex features to your Web pages. When you use Spry, you are adding Ajax, which is a combination of XML and JavaScript that can be styled using CSS. Think of a widget as a special feature that is more advanced than most dialog boxes and other features in Dreamweaver. With widgets, you can create complex features, such as drop-down menus, collapsible panels, tabbed panels, and more.

continued

Using the Properties inspector, you can enter names for all the items and subitems in the Spry menu bar.

You can also add or remove items and subitems.

Create a Drop-Down Menu *(continued)*

⓬ Type a name in the **Text** field.

⓭ Press Enter (Return).

● The name appears in the workspace and in the Properties inspector.

⓮ Repeat steps **11** to **13** for the other subitems of Item 1.

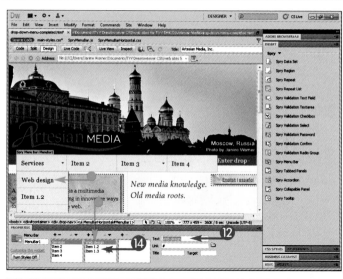

⓯ Repeat steps **8** to **14**, replacing all the item and subitem names with the text for your navigation menu.

⓰ Click ⊞ to add an item or subitem.

● A new item or subitem appears in the Properties inspector and the workspace.

● You can click ⊟ to remove any selected item or subitem.

⑰ Click any menu item or subitem that you want to turn into a link.

⑱ Type the URL in the **Link** field.

⑲ Press Enter (Return).

● You can click 📁 to browse to find any page in your site and set the link.

The item or subitem is linked, and the URL appears in the Link field in the Properties inspector when it is selected.

⑳ Click **File** and then click **Save**.

The page is saved, and Dreamweaver automatically creates a collection of special files that make the drop-down menu work.

Note: These files are saved in a folder named Spry that Dreamweaver creates in your local root folder. This folder must be uploaded to your Web server when you publish your site for the drop-down menu to work. Do not change the name or move the location of this folder.

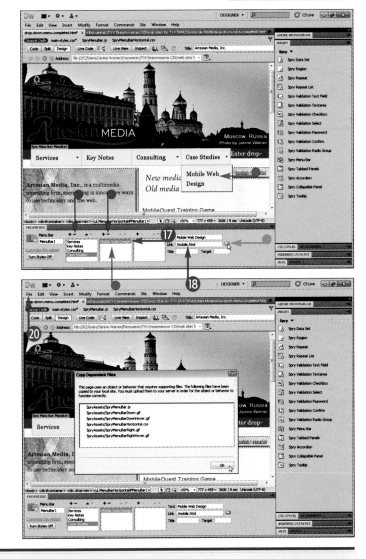

 TIPS

What are Spry validation widgets?
The Spry validation widgets are designed to work with Web forms to add validation features, such as confirmation that a check box has been selected or that a password has been entered properly.

 You must check the box to continue

Can I add more widgets and extensions to Dreamweaver?
Yes. Adobe hosts a Developer's section on its Web site where programmers can offer widgets and other add-ons for Dreamweaver. Some widgets are free; others cost money. You can learn more about widgets and extensions and download add-ons for Dreamweaver at www.adobe.com/devnet/dreamweaver/.

Edit a Drop-Down Menu

After you have added a drop-down menu to your site, you will want to change the appearance to better match the design on your Web pages. You can edit the colors, fonts, and other features of a drop-down menu by editing the corresponding CSS rules.

Edit a Drop-Down Menu

Note: Add a drop-down menu, as shown in the previous section, "Create a Drop-Down Menu," and then follow these steps.

1. Click **Window**.

2. Click **CSS Styles**.

● The CSS Styles panel opens.

3. Click + to open the style sheet that corresponds to the Spry menu.

● The Spry menu opens, and all the styles that control the appearance of the menu are listed in the CSS Styles panel.

● You can click once on any style name to view and edit the definition in the CSS Styles panel's Properties pane.

● Click here and drag to expand the Properties pane.

4. Double-click the name of the style that you want to edit.

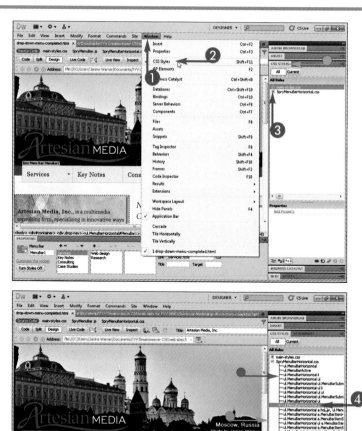

The selected style opens in the CSS Rule Definition dialog box.

5 Click to select a category.

6 Make your changes to the style.

Note: In this example, the background color is changed.

● You can click **Apply** to preview the changes.

7 Click **OK**.

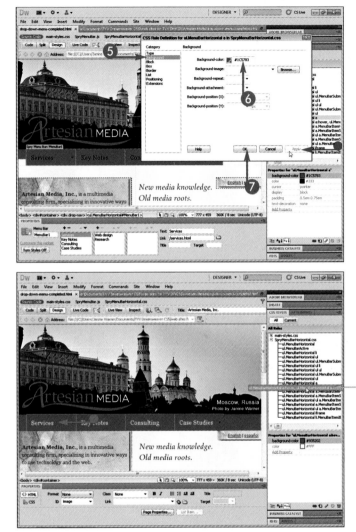

The style change is reflected in the workspace.

● In this example, the background color of the drop-down menu was changed to blue, and the text color was changed to white.

● Click any other style to edit it in the Properties pane or double-click to open it in the CSS Rule Definition dialog box.

 TIP

How do I know which style corresponds to the menu items?

When you click the name of a style in the CSS Styles panel, the rule is displayed in the Properties pane. By studying the style definition rules, you can deduce which style controls which formatting element. For example, click the style named **ul.MenuBarHorizontal a**, and you can see that the style controls the background color, text color, cursor display, and padding for the active link style, which controls how any linked text appears when the page is first loaded into a Web browser.

Menu Items
Background color
Text color
Cursor display
Padding

Create Tabbed Panels

Dreamweaver's Tabbed Panels widget, available from the Spry menu, makes it easy to add a set of panels that can be changed by clicking the tabs at the top of the panel set. Because the Spry widget uses Ajax, the Web page does not have to be reloaded for the panels to change when a user clicks a tab.

Create Tabbed Panels

Note: If the Insert panel is not open, click **Window** and then click **Insert** to open it.

1. Click to place your cursor where you want to add the panel set.

2. Click ▾ in the Insert panel.

3. Click **Spry**.

The Spry Insert panel appears.

4. Click **Spry Tabbed Panels**.

A Spry tabbed panel appears in the workspace.

 Click the blue Spry tabbed panels bar.

● The tabbed panel bar properties appear in the Properties inspector.

⑥ Click ➕.

● A new tab is added to the panel group.

● Click a tab in the Properties inspector and click ▲ to move the tab up or ▼ to move it down.

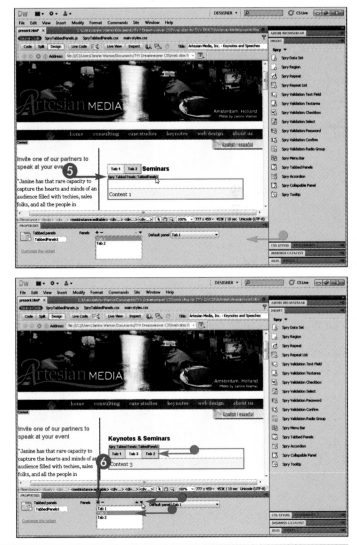

Can I add as many panels as I want?

Yes. But keep in mind that the more panels you include, the more space the panel group will take up in the browser, and the longer the page will take to download. Limiting a panel group to no more than eight items is a good practice.

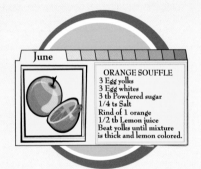

Add Content to Tabbed Panels

You can edit the text in the panels and tabs of a tabbed panel group in Dreamweaver's workspace. You can also insert images, video, and other elements into the panels.

Add Content to Tabbed Panels

Note: *Insert a tabbed panel group, as shown in the previous section, "Create Tabbed Panels," and then follow these steps.*

1 Click and drag to select the text on a tab.

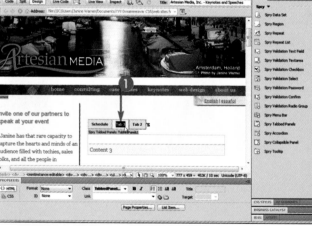

2 Type to enter new text on the tab.

3 Repeat steps **1** and **2** for each tab.

4 Click the blue Spry tabbed panels bar.

⑤ Click the name of a tab to select the panel.

● The selected panel is displayed in the workspace.

⑥ Enter any text, images, or other elements that you want in the tab area.

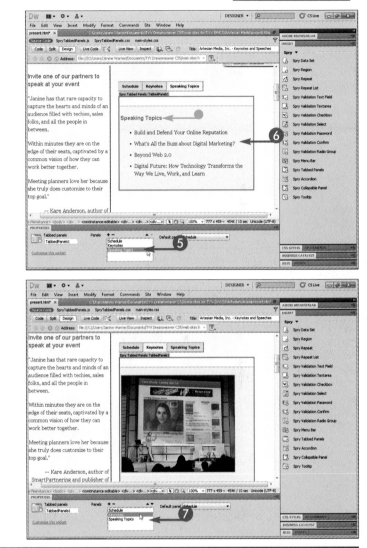

The new content is displayed in the panel in Dreamweaver's workspace.

⑦ Repeat steps **4** to **6** for each panel.

TIP

Can I add multimedia to tabbed panels?

Yes. You can insert anything into a panel that you can insert into a Web page, and you do so in much the same way. Just make sure that you have selected the panel in which you want to add content in the Properties inspector while you have the blue Spry tabbed panels bar selected.

Edit Tabbed Panels

You can edit the appearance of tabbed panels by editing the corresponding style rules. By editing the styles, you can change the color, font, and other attributes of the panels and tabs.

Edit Tabbed Panels

Note: Insert a tabbed panel group and add content to it, as shown in the previous two sections, and then follow these steps.

① Click **Window**.

② Click **CSS Styles**.

● The CSS Styles panel opens.

③ Click + to open the style sheet that corresponds to the tabbed panels.

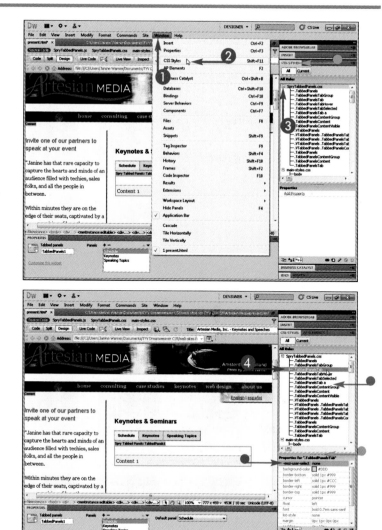

● The styles that control the appearance of the tabbed panels are opened and listed in the CSS Styles panel.

● You can click once on any style name to view and edit the definition in the CSS Styles panel's Properties pane.

● Click here and drag to expand the Properties pane.

④ Double-click the name of the style that you want to edit.

The selected style opens in the CSS Rule Definition dialog box.

⑤ Click a category.

⑥ Make your changes to the style.

Note: In this example, the background color is changed from a light gray color to a light blue color.

● You can click **Apply** to preview the changes.

⑦ Click **OK**.

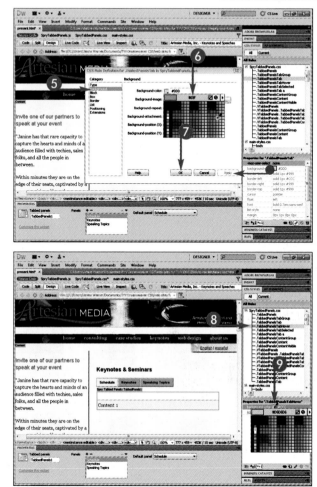

The style change is reflected in the workspace.

⑧ Click the name of another style that you want to edit.

⑨ Edit the selected style in the Properties pane.

Note: In this example, the tab color is changed.

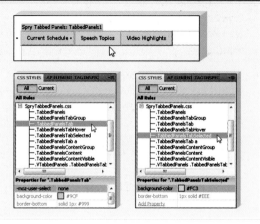

TIP

Can I use different colors for selected tabs?

Yes. The Spry panel tabs have separate styles for each of the three active link states: Tab, Tab Selected, and Tab Hover. You can specify different colors for each setting.

In this example, the Tab style is light blue, which will make links that are not actively selected light blue.

The Tab Selected style is an orange color. The tab for the selected section is displayed in the selector color.

Link styles can include different background colors, fonts, borders, and other variations to create attractive menu bars.

The Tab Hover style appears only when a user rolls the cursor over a tab.

Using the Open Browser Window Behavior

You can launch a new browser window with the click of a link, and you can specify the height and width of the new window to perfectly fit video and images in their own viewers or add other additional information, such as definitions.

Using the Open Browser Window Behavior

① Click an image, selection of text, or other element that you want to serve as the trigger for the behavior.

② Click **Window**.

③ Click **Behaviors**.

● The Behaviors pane opens in the Tag Inspector panel.

④ Click ▼.

The list of behaviors is displayed.

⑤ Click **Open Browser Window**.

Note: You can select other behaviors from the list to apply those features.

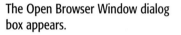

The Open Browser Window dialog box appears.

⑥ Click **Browse**.

The Select File dialog box opens.

⑦ Click ▾ and select the folder with the page to which you want to link.

⑧ Click the file.

⑨ Click **OK**.

You are returned to the Open Browser Window dialog box.

⑩ Type the width in pixels.

● If you leave the height blank, the window will expand to fill the content automatically.

⑪ Click any attributes that you want to include (☐ changes to ☑).

⑫ Type a name.

Note: You cannot use spaces or special characters.

⑬ Click **OK**.

TIP

What is the difference between behavior events and actions?

Think of an event in a behavior like a match and the action like the flame on a candle. When you use a behavior on your Web page, you get to choose what kind of event you want to serve as the spark. One common choice is `onClick`, which triggers the action of a behavior when a user clicks a link. Another common choice is `onMouseOver`, which triggers the action of a behavior when a user rolls the cursor over a link.

continued

After you add a behavior, you can specify the event that will trigger the action of the behavior. With the Open Browser Window behavior, both the `onClick` and `onMouseOver` events are good choices.

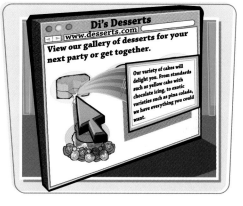

Using the Open Browser Window Behavior *(continued)*

⑭ Click here.

Note: *Hint: Click just inside the line.*

　　▣ appears.

⑮ Click ▣.

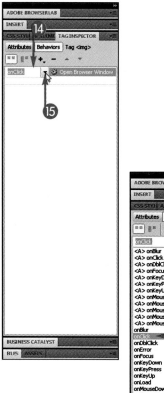

The drop-down list of functions appears.

⑯ Click an event to serve as the trigger for the behavior.

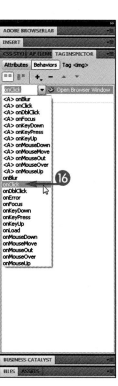

- The event name is displayed in the Behaviors panel and is associated with the behavior.

⑰ Click to preview the page in a Web browser.

⑱ Click a browser.

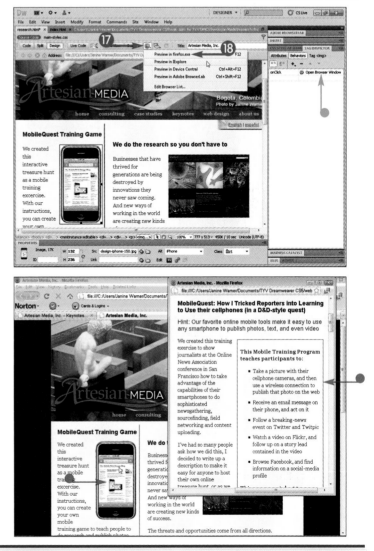

The page opens in the Web browser that you selected.

- When you perform the trigger on the element, such as click the image, the new browser window opens in the specified size.

Can I link images, text, and other types of files to behaviors?

Just about anything you can use for a link in Dreamweaver you can associate with a behavior. Just select any image, section of text, or even a video or animation file and then click to select the Behavior action and events from the Behaviors panel.

Index

Index

Index

Index

Index

Index

Read Less–Learn More®

Visual®

There's a Visual book for every learning level…

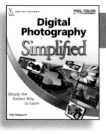

Simplified®

The place to start if you're new to computers. Full color.

- Computers
- Creating Web Pages
- Digital Photography
- Internet
- Mac OS
- Office
- Windows

Teach Yourself VISUALLY™

Get beginning to intermediate-level training in a variety of topics. Full color.

- Access
- Bridge
- Chess
- Computers
- Crocheting
- Digital Photography
- Dog training
- Dreamweaver
- Excel
- Flash
- Golf
- Guitar
- Handspinning
- HTML
- iLife
- iPhoto
- Jewelry Making & Beading
- Knitting
- Mac OS
- Office
- Photoshop
- Photoshop Elements
- Piano
- Poker
- PowerPoint
- Quilting
- Scrapbooking
- Sewing
- Windows
- Wireless Networking
- Word

Top 100 Simplified® Tips & Tricks

Tips and techniques to take your skills beyond the basics. Full color.

- Digital Photography
- eBay
- Excel
- Google
- Internet
- Mac OS
- Office
- Photoshop
- Photoshop Elements
- PowerPoint
- Windows

...all designed for visual learners—just like you!

Master VISUALLY®

Your complete visual reference. Two-color interior.

- 3ds Max
- Creating Web Pages
- Dreamweaver and Flash
- Excel
- Excel VBA Programming
- iPod and iTunes
- Mac OS
- Office
- Optimizing PC Performance
- Photoshop Elements
- QuickBooks
- Quicken
- Windows
- Windows Mobile
- Windows Server

Visual Blueprint™

Where to go for professional-level programming instruction. Two-color interior.

- Ajax
- ASP.NET 2.0
- Excel Data Analysis
- Excel Pivot Tables
- Excel Programming
- HTML
- JavaScript
- Mambo
- PHP & MySQL
- SEO
- Ubuntu Linux
- Vista Sidebar
- Visual Basic
- XML

Visual Encyclopedia™

Your A to Z reference of tools and techniques. Full color.

- Dreamweaver
- Excel
- Mac OS
- Photoshop
- Windows

Visual Quick Tips

Shortcuts, tricks, and techniques for getting more done in less time. Full color.

- Crochet
- Digital Photography
- Excel
- Internet
- iPod & iTunes
- Knitting
- Mac OS
- MySpace
- Office
- PowerPoint
- Windows
- Wireless Networking

Visual®
An Imprint of ⊕**WILEY**
Now you know.